GET THAT JOB!

GET THAT JOB!

The complete, thorough, hands-on guide to the whole recruitment and selection process – for graduates and ambitious executives in early career...

ANDY GIBB

Viva Books

New Delhi | Mumbai | Chennai | Kolkata | Bengaluru | Hyderabad | Kochi | Guwahati

First Indian Edition 2010

VIVA BOOKS PRIVATE LIMITED

- 4737/23 Ansari Road, Daryaganj, New Delhi 110 002
  E-mail: vivadelhi@vivagroupindia.net, Tel. 42242200
- 76, Service Industries, Shirvane, Sector 1, Nerul, Navi Mumbai 400 706
  E-mail: vivamumbai@vivagroupindia.net, Tel. 27721273, 27721274
- Jamals Fazal Chambers, 26 Greams Road, Chennai 600 006
  E-mail: vivachennai@vivagroupindia.net, Tel. 28290304, 28294241
- B-103, Jindal Towers, 21/1A/3 Darga Road, Kolkata 700 017
  E-mail: vivakolkata@vivagroupindia.net, Tel. 22836381, 22816713
- 7, Sovereign Park Apartments, 56-58, K. R. Road, Basavanagudi, Bengaluru 560 004
  E-mail: vivabangalore@vivagroupindia.net, Tel. 26607409, 26607410
- 101-102 Mughal Marc Apartments, 3-4-637 to 641, Narayanguda, Hyderabad 500 029
  E-mail: vivahyderabad@vivagroupindia.net, Tel. 27564481, 27564482
- Beevi Towers, First Floor, SRM Road, Kaloor, Kochi 682 018, Kerala
  E-mail: vivakochi@vivagroupindia.net, Tel: 0484-2403055, 2403056
- 232, GNB Road, Beside UCO Bank, Silpukhuri, Guwahati 781 003
  E-mail: vivaguwahati@vivagroupindia.net, Tel: 0361-2666386

www.vivagroupindia.com

Published by arrangement with
How to Books
Spring Hill House, Spring Hill Road
Begbroke, Oxford OX5 1RX,
United Kingdom

NOTE: The material contained in this book is set out in good faith for general guidance and no liability can be accepted for loss or expense incurred as a result of relying in particular circumstances on statements made in the book. The laws and regulations are complex and liable to change, and readers should check the current position with the relevant authorited before making personal arrangements.

ISBN : 978-81-309-1463-3

Published by Vinod Vasishtha for Viva Books Private Limited, 4737/23, Ansari Road, New Delhi-110 002. Printed and bound by Swan Press, New Delhi.

M0000

Contents

Appendices

Preface

As you open this book, what are you looking for?

Are you self-assured, idealistic, tech-savvy and already have expectations about the work and lifestyle you want, but would welcome clear inside track information to help you get there?

Or you may be a little anxious, keen to make the right choices but not sure what these should be or how best to go about it. You want a structure to help you choose a career, and complete guidance on how best to get through the selection processes; also examples of cvs, interviews, assessment centres and psychometric tests to practise on.

Or have you a friend or relative who has to make career decisions and pass important interviews? They may not listen to every suggestion, but you would like them to have access to clear impartial advice to help them arrive at the best decisions for themselves.

This book aims to provide you with everything you need to help you achieve the lifestyle you want by getting the right job for you. It is for people who are trying to get it right, whose sensitivity, ambition and natural impatience in today's plugged-in multi-tasking life requires quick answers, accessible interfaces, respect and consideration. Work and university are increasingly challenging yet team-oriented and diverse and less focused on long-term commitments. A job is judged by how it fits your desired lifestyle, contributes to others, and how much value it adds to your skill set, and résumé/cv.

Organisations are increasingly aware that they will survive and thrive, or fail depending on how successful they are in attracting and recruiting the right people to fit into their teams, be motivated by the task at hand and achieve their full potential so that the organisation can itself achieve its goals.

My goal in this book is to put together people and organisations. The advice and recommendations given are based on real situations, real people, real résumés and cvs, real interviews and assessment centres in the UK, the USA, the Netherlands, Australia, Asia, Africa and in many other countries around the world.

So where does my expertise come from? Well, I began my working life as a psychologist, first in Britain then on a Fulbright Scholarship to the USA. I became a business executive for one of the largest multinational energy corporations in the UK, Middle East and Asia, and recruited staff for a new business venture in Malaysia. As a chartered occupational (business) psychologist I have designed and run hundreds of interviews and assessment centres in four continents for new graduates and experienced staff, both technical and financial (and trained the interviewers and assessors). I have designed testing and screening processes for thousands of résumés/cvs, and as a head-hunter interviewed hundreds of people for senior positions.

Finally I headed up a worldwide recruitment business, leading recruitment staff in the USA, Europe, Asia and Australia, and researched the crucial factors that make the difference between high-flyers and those who may find more satisfaction in their work but will not be promoted as fast. I have counselled executives and students who are seeking to develop their careers and who want to achieve their desired lifestyles.

In addition, I have held discussions with the graduate recruiters of many of the top organisations, and been on the committee of business psychologists who prepare the annual conferences in Britain. Most recently I have been employed by one of the largest and best professional services firms in the world, working with head-hunters and researchers to recruit partners to expand their international operation.

All of that experience forms the basis of this book. You can read through the whole book from start to finish, or skip through it picking out those bits that you need at the time. Useful websites are included in Appendix 12 if you need to go deeper or to practise – some are excellent but not well known.

Andy Gibb
Langwaki, Malaysia

1
Why this book will enable you to do better at interview and selection

Our whole life is to a significant extent determined by interviews and other techniques used to select who will have this job or that contract. Two people with more or less identical experience and talent may present themselves for interview, and one will get the job or contract, not because their experience or talent are any better, but rather because they are better at presenting themselves and making sure that all their positive attributes are fully taken into account by those doing the selection.

And of course, up to a point, this skill in presenting themselves well **is** an additional talent that will probably enable them to be more successful in the job, and later to gain more responsibility and promotions.

So skill in being interviewed is an important, even critical one to acquire if we want to get ahead, achieve our full potential, and lead a happy and fulfilled life. But is this skill instinctive, inbuilt, something we either have or haven't?

Are some people naturally better at being interviewed?

Well, I would not have written this book if I thought this skill is 100 per cent instinctive, something we are either born with or not. I have seen far too many people who **think** they have a natural talent for interviews, who do not take the trouble to present themselves well. They prepare little, if at all, fail to take the advice available, enter the room, talk a lot in a charming way – and all too often fail completely.

'A no-hoper,' the interviewer will sigh as the candidate leaves the room. 'They didn't know what they wanted, didn't know what **we** wanted, hadn't thought through what skills and experience they had to offer, and didn't listen. A shame, they looked quite good on paper.'

Why résumés are so important

Of course, the interview is not the first stage of the selection process. Many people fail even to get an interview because their résumé, cv, covering letter, online application form or online psychometrics are not presented well enough, or do not do them justice. So this book also covers all these aspects, including especially how to prepare a résumé that gives you the best chance of securing an interview; and advice on filling in the increasingly common (and time-consuming) on-line application forms.

Assessment centres

Neither is the interview always the last stage of selection. Organisations have a whole menu of final selection devices available to them, some of which are quite lengthy and involved, and which if carried out properly give them a better chance of choosing a good (if not always the best) candidate. Assessment centres offer a series of different exercises designed to be similar to the real work you will be doing, and to give you the best opportunity to exhibit the competencies required. Development centres offer essentially the same thing, but are designed for staff already in the organisation, with the focus being on development as well as selection. So this book also covers assessment centres, development centres, group discussions, work simulation and other similar exercises. There's also more on psychometrics, and a look at selection processes when you already have significant work experience and/or are applying for selection (often promotion) within your current organisation.

What is the right career?

But are you applying for the job or organisation that is best for you? You don't want to go through a lot of effort to get a job, only to discover a month, a year, ten or 30 years too late that it was wrong (or at least significantly sub-optimal) for you. So this book also looks at how you can help yourself to choose the best range of jobs and organisations to apply for, or at least consider.

Organisational culture

The choices that organisations make will be influenced by their culture, and especially by their parent organisation. So for example, an American, British, Japanese or German organisation may well choose in very different ways from each other, even if they are all operating in a similar field. They will probably expect you to present yourself in different ways, and will concentrate on different aspects of your experience. This is a huge field; in the book we will cover some important aspects.

Head-hunters

Head-hunting is a very common way to fill many senior jobs, and we may well be approached by someone, often on the telephone, who asks whether we would be interested in a particular job 'that they think would be just right for us'. This book covers that process, and how best to manage these approaches. Such knowledge is important, even early on in a career, because we can shape our experience to some extent to make ourselves more marketable.

When you have to select . . .

And as we get more experienced, we will find ourselves in the position of being the person doing the selection. This book gives you insights into some of the pitfalls in selection, and some of the best ways to get the right person to help your team succeed.

Go straight to the chapter you need!

This book has been written so that you can go straight to the chapter that interests you – do not feel you have to start at the beginning. So if you are particularly interested in interviews, go straight to Chapter 10, Résumés (cvs) go to Chapter 7, Assessment Centres, see Chapter 13 and so on. Where there are useful links to other chapters, they are mentioned. The book deals with Career Choice (Chapter 2), how organisations decide who they want (Chapters 3–6), then the various selection methods they use (Chapters 7–15). Chapter 18 talks about head-hunters – otherwise known as executive search – because some organisations are even using head-hunter techniques at graduate recruitment, and it is certainly useful for the ambitious executive to know about this approach. Finally, there are some examples and other useful sources.

If you have comments, questions or personal experience concerning selection, email me at *andymgibb@yahoo.co.uk*

2
What do you really want to do?

What do you really, **really** want to do?

As a psychologist, I am used to asking clients questions like this, and waiting while they search around for something that really matters to them. Often the day to day stresses of business or home or college life dominate, and clients talk about achieving this year's targets, or gaining promotion; or getting a good degree or sorting out the children, garden or yard. And I wait, like a cat about to pounce (except that sounds predatory which I am not), with the next question: Why?

Because in my experience, no-one really, **really** wants to achieve this year's targets. They may be a means to an end, but except in clinically obsessive cases, not an end in themselves. And even if they achieved the promotion or the perfect degree, child, garden or yard, the satisfaction seldom lasts very long, and is replaced by a fear of slipping back next year, so there must be a deeper need somewhere hidden.

Your own personal strategy

Seasoned executives who can analyse a strategy plan in fine detail within a few hours, and list ten reasons why every corporation without one would drift aimlessly and amount to nothing, find that their own personal strategy amounts to . . . well, they haven't actually given it a lot of thought, could they have a bit more time on that one?

And sometimes they come out with what every hero in a John Grisham novel wants – to buy a sailing boat and sail away somewhere, 'but that's impossible just now, wait another ten or 20 years until I have more money' (or, in the novels, steal a few million or murder someone for their inheritance).

And I ask, 'Why?' again. And again, until we start to get to the point where they say something like: 'Well, there isn't a why, that is just what I really want.'

And I explore this with them for a while, and fine tune it some more, and we identify the blocks they perceive, skills they need to acquire, and why they feel they can't do it now, why they have to wait one or five or 20 years. And as they talk, they start to get energised and work out . . . what they really, really want, and once that is clear it usually doesn't need all the money, or the time, or all the anguish, all it needs is to focus on a few key issues like the people who really matter to them, and what they genuinely enjoy doing and are good at, just as in the best strategic plans.

2.1 MONEY, INCOME AND HAPPINESS

Money often looms as a key need for people. But it is being increasingly demonstrated in ground-breaking psychological research that money by itself does not make people happier. (Maybe this is why people say that psychology is all about proving what is obvious to everyone else.) True, people with money are more likely to be happy than people who have very little money, but provided you have about the average amount of money compared to people around you, studies are demonstrating that you are likely to be as happy as anyone who has millions or billions. The key issue (apart from genetics, which you can't do much about) is who you compare yourself with, and whether you genuinely believe you are making the most of yourself. So, if you compare yourself only with the people who are earning in the top 1 per cent, and you are not there, you will probably not be happy. But if you compare yourself with people around you at work, at home and at leisure, you will very probably find that your income is about the same as theirs – perhaps even a little bit higher.

If you concentrate on this, and on enjoying the work you are doing, then you are far more likely to be happy than if you are trying desperately to get a job which pays more money. Happiness is about enjoying the journey, it's not a destination in itself. That sounds glamorous but probably isn't. (For more on this, see the work of Professor Martin Seligman at the University of Pennsylvania, a leading expert on happiness. See *www.ppc.sas.upenn.edu*.)

The positive aspect of this is that it is up to you. You can choose the high-stress, high-pay job or career, and you may well find the work itself intensely satisfying. You need to recognise that you will be setting yourself new and ever more demanding targets (or having others set them for you), trying mightily to achieve them, and being developed into roles that you may not feel comfortable in. The rewards may be sufficient to motivate you when the going gets tough. However, you may also choose a job or career that you enjoy that does not have the same degree of stress, that pays adequately, even fairly well, and enables you to compare yourself with others in similar positions. You may not have the same status, or make the same impact on others, but you may well be happier and more fulfilled. You decide. That is what strategy is all about.

2.2 ARE YOU A HIGH-FLYER?

People in their 20s and 30s have significantly high energy levels, and maybe that's why most successful sportsmen and women are in their 20s and retire from active competition at the highest level in their early 30s. Young people are also quite properly ambitious. If you don't start out with high ambitions, you may end up achieving significantly less than you are capable of. In later life you could find yourself regretting that you did not aim higher; perhaps even struggling to find the resources to enable you to enjoy a healthy, satisfying lifestyle. So it is natural for many people to aim for the top, to go for the high-pay, high-achievement job or career, looking to reap the material rewards such positions promise. Be aware though, that your aspirations are likely to be increasing as fast as, or faster than, your income.

After some years of work, most people will be starting to get some feedback on how well they are doing, and an appreciation of how fast their career is progressing. Most organisations try to identify fast-track achievers or high-flyers by the time they are 30, and most professional services firms aim to make the best people partners in their 30s (the usual age varies by country and by profession; law for example is often earlier, accountancy slightly later). One of the reasons for identifying high-flyers is to ensure that they get the development experience that will benefit them in more challenging and senior roles, and also to some extent to ensure that they get the competitive remuneration to keep them with the organisation. If you are regarded as a 'high-flyer' you will probably be made aware of it, although some organisations are surprisingly reticent about this – partly because if they tell some people they are high-flyers, those who are not so identified may be de-motivated and leave, and partly because it can be seen as a self-fulfilling prophecy.

There have been many studies of high-flyers, often producing different answers. However, some of the better predictors of high-flyers are early responsibility, early experience in a variety of challenging situations – for example abroad, or in differing roles, and good networking skills.

Do you really want to fly high?

If you seem to be recognised as a high-flyer, only you know the effort and sacrifices you are having to put in to be successful. If you are enjoying life – the adrenaline highs, the sense of achievement, the praise, rewards – and can cope with the challenges and increasing demands placed on you, fine. But if you are increasingly finding yourself overstressed, feeling vulnerable, not enjoying work or life as much as you would like, then it is important to be aware that there are alternative paths which may make you happier as well as less stressed. This could involve a career change, or as likely a change of perspective.

If by this time you have a family or partner, or people close to you, you will benefit from involving them – after all, it is to some extent your understanding of their expectations that is driving you. If you talk to them about your situation you may well find that their expectations are more relaxed than you think, and that they regard being able to spend quality time with you as more important than your achieving another promotion. And don't think this need to change perspective won't happen to all the other high flyers – they will almost certainly come to the same choice of career change or change of perspective. For some this may come a bit later (by which time it could be more difficult to change career or to change perspective or expectations), and they may have missed some of the most important times in life, such as spending time with their young children, or enjoying active leisure activities, or even the next can't-miss business opportunity.

2.3 CAREER CHOICE – AND THE POSSIBILITY OF CHANGE

Your choice of career, or expertise you want to acquire, or next significant job, will probably have more effect on your life than any other single decision, except possibly your choice of partner. And in a funny way, your choice of employer is similar to a choice of partner (but don't tell them that!). Because you need someone you will enjoy being with, who will help you achieve your potential, who will support you when you encounter difficulties, and who will provide you with financial income for at least some of the time.

It is also a lot easier to get into an organisation when there is a good fit between what you want and offer and what they want, and what they offer. And don't be put off by the word 'career'. In earlier times, it is true, it was much more difficult to change jobs, even more difficult if not impossible to change employers, and a career really was for life – or at least it was, provided that your employer decided to make it that way. Even today in Japan, many salaried jobs are considered to be for life.

But in most other countries, there is much greater likelihood of being able to change jobs, employers and area of work. As the rate of change in jobs increases, so the value of previous experience decreases, making it easier for an employee who can learn fast to be as good and effective within weeks as one who has been around for years.

Making change work for you

This means that you can try a particular line of work, and if you do not like it or it is not giving you the rewards (financial and non-financial) you want, or if your employer has to cut back their staffing, then you can change, and within a few months have a reasonable chance of getting into a new line.

This does not mean that you should jump from one career to another every few years (unless this is what you particularly want to do). Most employers and most clients favour people who have some depth of experience, and once you have found the career line that suits you, you should find yourself motivated to develop yourself, develop new ways of working, and new services to offer clients. This is likely to be more satisfying than switching from one job to another.

So how do you go about deciding what you want to do? Well, there are a number of approaches, any one of which will do, because the crucial thing is thinking through all the angles, being brutally honest with yourself about yourself, and doing some research about the world of opportunities out there.

2.4 THREE CRUCIAL FACTORS THAT DETERMINE CAREER CHOICE

You need to take into consideration just three factors when making your choice of career:

- *Where do I want to work?* For example, in the country or in a city, and if so, which city, which country or continent? Do you want to work close to someone – your partner or potential partner perhaps?
- *Which type of industry or business do I want to work in?* For example do you want to work in government, or NGO, professional services like accountancy, consultancy, law, medicine, banking, energy or mining, communications, information technology, leisure or sports, water or other utilities, retail stores or logistics, transport, military, not for profit, etc.
- *What sort of role or particular job do I want?* This may be already largely defined by your choice of industry or business. For example, if you choose medicine, there are some well defined roles in that area such as doctor, nurse, and paramedic. But there are also some less obvious roles, such as accountant, administrator, receptionist, care assistant, physiotherapist, and psychiatrist. So try to think outside the box, and don't limit yourself to obvious roles. If you do not want to work for someone else, perhaps you would like to run your own business?

The crucial factor in all this is finding out what you enjoy. And I don't mean just the type of work, but also the type of activities you enjoy – for example meeting people, helping people, analysing numerical problems, presenting a case, analysing strategic or more conceptual issues, writing, reading, learning new things, teaching others skills you have yourself. There are exercises in Chapter 3 to help you work out what are your underlying motivators – the sort of activities and environments that you find get you excited.

2.5 THE IMPORTANCE OF PLAN A, PLAN B AND PLAN C

There are quite literally thousands of possible careers and jobs. And even if you are currently in a career, you can still change – right up to the point when you stop working altogether. So while it makes sense to try to determine which career will give you the best chance of being happy and successful, there is no need to narrow your choices down to just one, and put all your eggs in one basket. For one thing, you may well not be accepted into your first choice career. Your second or third choice may be just as good, or better, in the long term – and even in the short and medium term.

So having a Plan B makes a lot of sense, and even a Plan C as well. You can develop them in parallel, checking out or exploring the ground as you go along, collecting information and skills that will be useful to you, and seeing just how practical it is for you to get into a particular industry or profession. This also means that if you receive a setback in one area – your Plan A – a rejection, or even a series of rejections perhaps, you have already progressed your Plan B to the stage where you will not miss crucial deadlines, and are in a good position to develop this instead.

3
Exercises to help you decide the career that's right for you

There are two places to start:

1 Your own strengths and skills; and your own weaknesses and lack of skills;

2 What you enjoy doing.

It is probably best to start with what you enjoy doing, since you can always train yourself to gain skills or overcome weaknesses if you really want to do something and enjoy doing it. Whereas if you don't enjoy something, you will never be really motivated to do it, and it may be better to try something else, no matter how good you feel you are at it (unless you have a strong sense of obligation).

If you start with what you are good at and not so good at, you may well find you are putting up barriers to various careers or jobs which in practice can be overcome – albeit not without effort.

3.1 ENJOYING WHAT YOU DO – IDENTIFY YOUR UNDERLYING MOTIVATORS

Here are some exercises designed to help you focus on what you enjoy.

Exercise 1 Start by asking what you really, *really* want to do

Allow yourself between one and eight activities or roles, or just things you like doing. They don't necessarily have to be work related – there is quite enough work generated by leisure or sport activities to make a career in this area quite a practical choice. If you find it difficult to think of what you really like doing try some of these activities:

- Look through some magazines (choose ones that you like) and just consider all the different activities and jobs that are described in them. Write down those that appeal to you.
- Look through some newspapers or websites or blogs, and do the same thing, identifying activities that interest you and that you almost instinctively believe you would enjoy doing.
- Cut out pictures from magazines and make a collage on a large piece of paper. Arrange the pictures you have chosen in a way that makes sense to you, then (if you can) explain it to a friend.
- Talk to a friend about what you want to do, or even admit that you are undecided. Ask them to help you to get your thoughts clear, and then start talking about some of the areas you have considered. If the friend is playing their role well, they will notice the areas where you start to get excited, and those where you sound bored, they will spot the areas where you are uncertain and haven't really thought things through, and they may well suggest ideas that haven't occurred to you. Don't be too influenced by their ideas; after all, it is **you** who have to do the job, but they may well mention some areas that you hadn't considered before.
- Think of all your friends and acquaintances. What jobs do they have, and do any of these sound right for you, or excite you? This is a particularly rich source of advice. People like being asked about the work they do, and you can learn a lot from them. There is also the additional benefit that if you decide you **do** want to aim for this particular job or career, they can almost certainly give you useful contacts and ideas about how to start.
- Forget about jobs altogether, and just think of what you like doing. Perhaps playing interactive games, or particular sports, or reading

particular types of book, or talking with friends about other people, or travelling, or partying. Be as specific as you can. Write these activities down.

- Look at the career guidance websites in Appendix 12. They include some really useful ones, such as one that identifies which are the jobs that graduates from different fields tend to progress to. There is also an assortment of salary surveys, if you want to find where to make your fortune. Many are American, but all will give you ideas, and anyway business is increasingly international!

Exercise 2 Now ask *why* you like doing these jobs or activities; why do they interest you?

Be really honest. Imagine someone is asking you that **why** question – in fact, if you can arrange this, it is excellent to have someone actually ask it. Many professional counsellors are paid well just to ask precisely that question, and help you to clarify your answers to it. But a friend or relative will probably do almost as well – better in some cases if you already trust them.

You may well find that there is an underlying reason why you enjoy these activities – perhaps you like not having a fixed schedule of work, or working out of doors, or meeting new people, or . . . If so, and you can get at the underlying enjoyment, then there may well be other jobs or careers or activities that will provide as much as or more enjoyment than any you have thought of so far.

Exercise 3 Get down to fundamentals

Carry on asking '**Why** do I enjoy doing these activities?' until you finally have to say, 'I just enjoy doing them, that's fundamentally what I find pleasure in doing.' There may be from one to ten or so of these. Write them down, and check again that they seem to be central to what you want.

Exercise 4 Discover your underlying motivators

If you still find it difficult, this is a powerful exercise to help you identify the underlying motivators that determine whether you like a job or not. Try this:

Write down four or five jobs or activities that you believe you would probably like most, and two or three that you think you would dislike. No need to be sure about this, the exercise will do everything else.

L1 Most liked: ______________________________

L2 Next most liked: ______________________________

L3 Next most liked : ______________________________

L4 Next most liked: ______________________________

L5 Next most liked: ______________________________

D1 Most disliked: ______________________________

D2 Next most disliked: ______________________________

D3 Next most disliked: ______________________________

Now take a pair of the liked activities, and one of the disliked, and ask yourself what the liked pair have in common that the disliked one does not have. For example, you might have liked accountant and lawyer, and disliked social worker. Some of the common factors that you might list for the two liked jobs that you think are lacking in the disliked one may be:

- professional services;
- working with business people;
- well paid;
- attention to detail, especially numerical;
- long hours;
- high pressure, lots of deadlines;
- opportunity to run your own business.

The important thing for the purposes of this exercise is not how accurate your assessment is (a social worker might disagree with some of the factors above) – it is getting at some of the underlying things you enjoy.

Do this again with another pair of liked jobs, and a different disliked one, until you have done most of the combinations.

For example, if L1 is the most liked job, L2 the second liked job and so on to L5, and D1 is the job you most dislike, D2 the job you dislike next and so on, compare them using these combinations:

What Lx and Ly have in common and Dz does not have is:

L1	L2	D1	
L3	L4	D2	
L1	L4	D1	
L2	L3	D2	
L1	L5	D3	
L3	L4	D3	

Even doing half this table would probably be enough, until you feel you are getting close to your final list, because the same characteristics keep coming up. Now combine the factors that are obviously so similar they are effectively the same. See Appendix 2 for an example of the five factors that a job seeker came up with (listed A–E).

You should end up with a list of four or five fairly general criteria which you are implicitly using to decide what jobs or activities you enjoy. And as you look at this list (whichever method(s) you used to get to it) you may find other jobs occur to you that share these characteristics. For example, you might start to consider Human Resources, Analyst, Actuary, Insurance Broker, Real Estate . . .

Exercise 5 Use Google or Yahoo as a career search engine

Here's another exercise: think of as many activities that you enjoy as you can. Then put them in pairs into a search engine like Google, and see what comes out. Some of the responses will be irrelevant, but some will almost certainly contain jobs or careers that you might not otherwise have considered. Use the search engine to refine this list until you have something that you feel represents what you want.

Exercise 6 Check your criteria against real-life jobs

Now look through the list of 400-plus jobs and careers in Appendix 1 and score the most likely ones according to the criteria you have identified, based on the extent to which each one would be able to meet these criteria. Award a mark of 5 if you think the job is in the top 20% and you are very confident you would enjoy it most of the time, 4 if it is well above average, 3 for average, 2 for below average and 1 or 0 if it's in the lowest 20%. Be generous at first, and you should get a long list. Then go through this list again, being more rigorous, and you should begin to find certain jobs or careers starting to emerge. See Appendix 2 for an example of how the rating might look – maybe the list is the same as you started with, but probably with quite a few new jobs to consider. And you should have a better appreciation of why you like these types of jobs, and therefore what you really enjoy.

3.2 WHAT ARE YOU REALLY GOOD AT?

Examine your own skills and aptitudes. What are your strengths and weaknesses compared to others? What do you do well, what activities do you frankly struggle with? You may be as specific or as general as you want here. You may identify *subjects*, eg maths or science or art or languages; or computing, or technology; or *activities*, eg routine work, creative work, making presentations, or selling anything to other people; or you may identify *specific jobs*, eg accountant, lawyer, supervisor, engineer, salesman, logistician.

Try to think in terms of competencies. Competency is a word used to describe the skills that someone needs to perform a job to the standard required. So the job of an engineer for example may be analysed into the different competencies required – perhaps competency in numerical analysis, thermodynamics, selection of suitable materials, and also contract management, cost-benefit analysis and communication. Competencies focus on skills that have to be exhibited, rather than qualifications or knowledge which may be old or irrelevant or simply not used. You may find that many well-prepared advertisements define the competencies required for the job; and many organisations define the competencies required by senior managers.

You may use Exercise 4 above to get at some of the more underlying aspects. Psychometrics can also help here – for example, to help you find out if you tend to behave more like an introvert or an extrovert, or discover how well you score on numerical or verbal analysis, etc.

3.3 PLAN A

Now compare these strengths and weaknesses against the list of possible jobs that you think you might enjoy. Which jobs contain most of what you feel confident and strong about, and little of what you feel unconfident, or weak about? You may draw up a table or spreadsheet to help you get the message:

Activities/jobs I may enjoy	My strengths and positive factors	Concerns about specific abilities	
			Plan A
			Plan A
			Plan A
			Plan B
			Plan B
			Plan B
			Plan C
			Plan C
			Plan C

The top two or three jobs or activities will most likely be the focus of your Plan A; they are the jobs you will initially aim for. But you will probably be aware that it is not always easy answering the questions above; there is often significant doubt as to what the 'right' answer is. In any case, you may find it very difficult to gain entry into some of your chosen jobs, or deadlines may have passed. You deal with this possibility by developing a Plan B and a Plan C.

3.4 REALISM: PLAN B AND PLAN C

Just as you can't always control who you will or will not love, any more than you can make someone love you, you may find that realistically there are limits to what organisations or jobs you can get. You may decide that a particular job or career or organisation is just right for you, you are well suited, and yet . . . somehow it just does not work: your résumés are rejected; the interviews go well but never quite well enough; deadlines pass . . .

Just like a good business plan, your personal plan needs to recognise the possibility of setbacks, and contain a set of Plan B organisations or jobs or careers which you will try if you are unsuccessful with the first lot (contained in Plan A). And given that we do not have perfect knowledge of all these organisations, and our priorities change over time, you may well find that actually these other organisations or jobs or careers are in fact better than or as good as your first set of choices. So don't get stuck to one set of targets, be prepared for Plan B or even Plan C.

This is a variant on scenario strategic planning – asking 'What if?' questions, so that if the desired or expected outcome does not happen, you are at least mentally prepared for this, and are already in good shape to consider what to do, with your Plan B or C sketched out.

3.5 PROFESSIONAL CAREER COUNSELLORS

Of course, you can always go to a professional career counsellor, or someone who fulfils a similar function. And there are a number of psychometric tests that can help you get a better appreciation of what you want and would be good at. Given the importance of these decisions, you may well consider the cost to be more than justified. You can find career counsellors in Yellow Pages or equivalent. *www.eos.co.uk* is a website run by Dai Williams, a psychologist who specialises in career counselling who also does personal counselling, or just do a search on 'career counsellor' on Google or any search engine, or contact the National Association of Career Counsellors or psychologists in your county or district.

3.6 GOVERNMENT CAREERS ADVICE

Schools and local authorities often provide a service, but the organisation of them changes frequently, so ask around. *www.dfes.gov.uk/publications/youth* provides the latest in UK government thinking. In summary, the government wants to provide better support to young people as they make decisions about their careers, education, health and other issues. What is being proposed is clear minimum expectations of the information, advice and guidance (IAG) that each young person and their parents should receive. These would be:

- at age 11–12 (year 7): an introduction from a variety of people, including other pupils, to what is on offer within secondary school;
- at age 13–14 (year 9): support in considering post-14 choices and a personal session with an adviser if they or their parents need or want it. This would complement plans for a local 14–19 learning prospectus;
- throughout the teenage years: better help to think through post-16 options, personal, social and health issues and career choices; an easy-to-access, innovative and independent ICT service through which young people can access national and local information from a variety of sources, including through an easily navigable website, online advisers and a helpline.

Schools and colleges would be accountable for ensuring the well-being and maximum progression of all their pupils and students, including those with severe and complex learning difficulties. To support this the government is proposing to devolve responsibility for commissioning information, advice and guidance and the funding that goes with it, from the Connexions service to local authorities, working through children's trusts, schools and colleges to ensure that young people have a better service linked to the school curriculum and to pastoral care; that services are efficient and cost-effective; and that high-performing Connexions services are preserved.

In most cases children's trusts, schools and colleges should agree on new arrangements for commissioning information, advice and guidance locally. But where schools and colleges believe that local provision is poor, they would have the right to commission the service directly. These new arrangements should be in place by 2008. Local authorities would be responsible for commissioning information advice and guidance for young people who do not attend a school or college. The arrangements vary in different parts of the country (and between Scotland, Wales, England and Northern Ireland).

Students at university or college should receive information advice and guidance from the university or college, and people under 19 should also be able to get some advice from a local university, even if they have left college or higher education.

So in the UK you should be able to expect good-quality careers advice, provided the delivery of the service matches what is being promised. In other countries, check the local government websites, and local schools and universities.

4
How to find out what organisations look for

Most organisations have a list of general qualities or criteria they look for in their key employees – sometimes based on studies, sometimes on just a listing of what seems 'right'. These are not for specific jobs, they are a statement of the type of people the organisation wants to have. Examples of these qualities include leadership, analytical ability, communication, respect for others, drive, achievement orientation, business sense, integrity, customer orientation, team work, imagination, strategic sense (to spot the key strategic issues).

These qualities are likely to be different depending on the culture and nationality of the organisation. For example, American organisations tend to place more emphasis on impact, initiative and integrity; British organisations tend to place more emphasis on team work, communication and technical skills. Employees may be rated against these criteria in performance reviews, and the criteria or qualities may appear in the annual report, website or other PR literature.

Gaining an advantage

Clearly it gives you a significant advantage to know what the organisation you are applying to is looking for – if for no other reason than you can supply your best evidence to them, presented clearly so they can't miss it. It may also give you an idea if this is the organisation you want to join.

If you are looking a little way in the future – for example one year away, perhaps when you graduate, or recognise that you will want a career move – you can sometimes start a particular activity that you know will gain you credit. This is sometimes called building a résumé, or more nastily, résumé-padding. So if you recognise that the organisation places considerable value on team work, you may want to join a team or society, and undertake activities that will provide you with up-to-date and significant evidence of this.

I have already mentioned most of the sources that will give you clues on what the organisation looks for – annual report, website, PR literature, recruitment brochures – but if the organisation is big enough, a web search will probably produce enough stories from national or local newspapers to provide evidence on what they look for in their top employees. Of course, the best source is often someone who is already working there, so try to tap this source. But don't make it an interrogation – most people like talking about their place of work, but they will resent having a checklist of questions thrown at them. Relax, take some time, smile, be genuinely interested in what they are saying, and allow them to digress a bit from what you want – after all, they are providing you with valuable information. Your way of paying them back is to listen actively.

Asking for advice is an effective method of job seeking

It can even be a particularly effective way to secure a job – many Americans job seekers use this approach, contacting executives and asking questions about the organisation and the particular job they are interested in. The job seekers start out by saying that they are not looking for a job – but actually they are . . .

Advertisements

Of course, if you have a particular job in mind, the organisation should have spelled out at least some of the factors or qualifications they are looking for. This is the case whether you found the job on a website, or newspaper or internal board, or were contacted by a friend or a head-hunter . . . If they don't provide the job requirements then it is difficult to see how anyone can tell whether they are suited for the position or not, and it is entirely appropriate to ask for more information. It's also worth checking at this stage that your choice to apply to them is still sound and appropriate!

5
Advertisements

People sometimes think the best way to get a job or decide what career to go for is to apply to advertisements in newspapers, job posting websites, or anywhere else. It is certainly straightforward; at least in this way you know that the organisation has a requirement, and usually you have some idea of what they are looking for.

Or do you? Many governments, local authority employers, and NGOs (non-government organisations, like the UN for example) have policies that require them always to advertise vacancies, even if they already have a preferred candidate, who is almost guaranteed to get the job.

A very good and well-respected book on job search, *What color is your parachute?* (see Appendix 12) reckons that applying to advertisements is the exact reverse of the way you should go about getting a job, because it focuses on what **they** want, rather than what **you** want. If you allow yourself to be led by advertisements, you are likely to find yourself in jobs that for whatever reason are vacant at the time, and are unlikely to offer the sort of development and financial and non-financial rewards you want in the future.

Supply and demand

Advertisements do have a useful function – they can give you an idea of what sort of jobs are available out there, where the current supply is less than demand. But if you qualify for these jobs, you probably know this already. Some analysts use a count of the total number of advertisements in a given month as a crude measure of how 'buoyant' the labour market is.

The great majority of jobs are filled by other means than advertisements. So use advertisements as reminders of career paths that you may want to consider; think of them as indicators of where current supply is less than demand; and, just once in a while, as telling you of something that may be right for you.

Bargain?

But looking only at advertisements is like walking into a shop, not knowing what you want to buy, looking for all the special offers that the shop prominently advertises, picking one, two or three, and wondering a few days later why you bought something you didn't really need, or even want. Essentially you have let yourself be controlled or at least influenced into something that the organisation was having difficulty shifting – that is why they advertised or promoted it so prominently. And it's the same with recruitment advertisements. At least in part it comes down to the culture of the organisation.

Replying to advertisements

Replying to advertisements usually requires a résumé (cv) – this is certainly the most effective and quickest way to apply, either on paper or by email, depending on what the advertisement specifies. Or you may have to complete an online application form. Chapters 7 to 9 cover résumés, covering letters and online applications. But first it is worth giving some thought to the sort of organisation(s) you are applying to, including the culture of the organisation. This is the subject of the next chapter . . .

6
Cultural influences – are all organisations the same?

By cultural influences I mean the way an organisation thinks and works, apart from the technical or financial aspects. This will make a huge difference to whether or not you will fit in to the organisation. If you are not in tune with their way of working, and general approach to business, you will not be happy or successful in the position. Knowing the culture of the organisation therefore will not only give you an advantage in getting through the selection process, it may also indicate how likely you are to be happy and succeed there – indeed, whether it is worth applying at all.

For example, a locally based organisation with just a few sites in a small region will probably have a local culture, and will probably also reflect strongly the personality of the person or people who started it. This style may suit you or it may not – either way, in a smallish organisation you are going to be affected by it.

Multinationals

Multinational organisations with household names generally like to think that they have an international culture, but usually the division trading in each particular country will take care to present itself as a supporter of local values and business, and often be incorporated locally as well. However, multinationals always have some form of head office, and this will usually drive the corporate style and culture.

So if you are applying to an American multinational in Britain, you should expect (and will probably find) a blend of American culture and British style of doing business. The more senior the job you are applying for, the more likely the culture of the head office is going to be important. You will usually find out information about the organisation you are applying for as part of your normal research about the company. But it is also invaluable if you know, or can get into contact with, someone who is already working there.

Inside knowledge

If you do know someone, ask them about what it is like to work there, what seems to be well thought of, and what is considered wrong, or inappropriate. Are people expected to work long hours, or is there more of a concentration on delivering results, irrespective of the hours worked? Is team work considered a priority, or is the focus on individual effort? Does the organisation concentrate on domestic markets, or on international ones? And so on. If you do find the organisation interesting, many now encourage current employees to recommend people they know for positions – and provide an incentive for them to do so. If this is the case, then your friend may be even keener for you to apply.

If you do not know, and are unable to find, anyone who can help you with this, you can still get quite a lot of information from the Annual Report and other PR publications. If even this does not provide you with the information you need, it may be that the company genuinely does not have a guiding culture – unlikely but possible.

It is possible to make generalisations about organisations based on their size and the nationality of their head office. I have included some here, focusing especially on what these organisations are likely to expect from candidates for jobs, but remember that these are generalisations only, and it is much better to get real information from people working there. There are also a number of books and websites which research this aspect in more detail, and some of these are listed in Appendix 12. For example, *www.businessculture.com* provides good advice on business culture and etiquette in most countries, and *www.eurograduate.com/marketreports/culture-matters* includes neat, short summaries of what to expect in the different European countries. Geert Hofstede's analysis of business culture was one of the earliest and best: he identified five dimensions which differentiate the ways different cultures approach life. See *www.cyborlink.com* for example, or *www.geert-hofstede.com*

Punctuality

In all organisations you will need to be on time, or just ahead of time. While in some cultures punctuality is less important than, for instance, the proper completion of elaborate social rituals, as an applicant for a job you need to show respect for the organisation and people you are applying to, and be on time.

6.1 AMERICAN ORGANISATIONS

American-based organisations usually expect candidates to present themselves well in a confident and team-oriented way, and almost expect candidates to play up their record with perhaps a degree of exaggeration (but not lie). So, for example, they may expect résumés to be better and more elaborately formatted, a clear statement of what your career objective is, and perhaps for the résumé to be even more focused on their particular requirements. They sometimes like glowing letters of recommendation from people you have worked for or with (but not your present employers) – or at least their inclusion as references.

Partly for legal reasons they are unlikely to ask or to take into consideration your age, sex, race, or any issues that are not directly related to your competence to do the job in question (although you may find that children and family issues are discussed over a meal in an informal way). They may however ask you direct questions about your compensation in your current or previous jobs. (Compensation includes all the benefits you receive in addition to your salary, such as your pension, or a car.) American candidates have usually had significant preparation in marketing themselves and being interviewed and often prepare different résumés focused on specific organisations or skill sets. Many American résumés do not contain date of birth, marital status etc and application forms often do not ask for this. However, it may be needed for background checks. They will normally ask your permission for this. Don't include your social security number in your résumé because of the risk of identity theft. Similarly, date of graduation may give hints as to your age, but will be needed for the checks that will be done if you are being considered for a job. They will ask direct questions about your competencies and any practical issues relating to how you will manage your work, including customer care.

Increasingly, American companies are using electronic or optical scanning methods of collecting and screening résumés, so it is important that all job-related competencies that you have are clearly stated. American candidates may well send a thank you letter after an interview or assessment, including reminders of their key competencies, and why after the interview they think they are even better suited to the job in question. Ask for the business card of the person interviewing you to enable you to send a personal letter, accurately addressed.

American organisations tend to make quicker decisions on hiring, partly because they are also quicker to 'fire' or terminate employment. So the first six months is a trial period for both employer and employee. American first degrees are broader and less specialised than British degrees, for example, so British candidates will probably have deeper knowledge in their degree subject, but have covered fewer subjects in total.

6.2 CANADIAN ORGANISATIONS

Don't regard Canadian organisations as the same as US ones, although they also tend to measure success in terms of personal achievement, and have the same respect for individualism. Canadians are self-reliant and confident, but keep their private lives to themselves. The French-speaking part of Canada will tend to share more of the characteristics of French organisations.

6.3 FRENCH ORGANISATIONS

French organisations may well use more unusual methods of selecting, including particularly graphology (study of handwriting), so a hand-written covering letter may be called for. They are more interested in you as a complete person, and will be interested in any contacts you already have, as well as, of course, your competencies and knowledge of the French language. They use more gestures, and may well be less 'remote', but you need to respect their privacy. Be polite, well dressed, and show respect for authority – much French decision-making is hierarchical and centralised.

6.4 NETHERLANDS ORGANISATIONS

Netherlands organisations are likely to expect you to be relatively modest about your achievements – bragging or boasting is seen as offensive, and will not help you to get a job. In contrast, make sure that all your evidence, including positive perspective, is in your résumé, or online application, but don't use adjectives that make it seem that you are proud of your achievements. If the selector is good they will probe in a very direct manner to make sure they know clearly what you have done. So expect direct questioning – so direct it may almost appear rude. It isn't, it is just their style. Be direct back, but never aggressive.

6.5 GERMAN AND SWISS ORGANISATIONS

German and Swiss organisations are likely to be similar to those of the Netherlands (although both would deny it). The emphasis will be on hard evidence and academic and work achievements. Don't expect 'pointless' casual conversation. German candidates put a lot of effort into preparing long, elaborate factual résumés usually with a photo, and often expect or at least request that their résumés are returned. German companies are therefore used to probing résumés at length to test technical or professional competence, so expect this at interview.

6.6 BRITISH ORGANISATIONS

British organisations are likely to be a blend of American and European cultures. They will expect candidates to be able to present themselves confidently, and to have at least done some research about the organisation. Expect assessment centres for graduate recruitment for at least the larger organisations, particularly when they are recruiting for a graduate development programme. However, a number of organisations use assessment centre-type selection for quite senior positions – for example, partner recruitment into professional services. For current staff, these are usually called development centres, the idea being that every participant should gain some insights into their best avenue of development.

6.7 ASIAN ORGANISATIONS

Asian organisations are likely to place quite an emphasis on how well you will fit into their corporate culture, as well as on your competency. Expect some form of social event, eg dinner or drinks. They may tell you that this is not part of the assessment, but in all probability it is, because they will be very keen to see how well you would fit in, and how well they can 'trust' you. Quite possibly you will already have had some contact with them, and been considered someone they may be able to trust. In Japanese organisations, expect alcohol to flow freely, the assumption being that this makes candidates less inhibited, and more likely to tell the truth and to exhibit their 'real' behaviour. Other Asian cultures may be based on Islamic principles, and there will be no alcohol, but talk will still flow freely. These organisations may well place less emphasis on the individual, and more on collective group action, so be prepared to show how you support others, and work for the team, rather than necessarily standing out as an individual.

6.8 AUSTRALIAN ORGANISATIONS

Australians value individualism, and may well appear self-confident, but this is not always as deep-seated as you may think, so be careful of voicing direct criticism. However, they will expect you to have opinions and to defend these. Australians tend to be very tolerant regarding others' opinions and way of life, so for example travel is valued highly, and non-PC jokes may be expected. Differing orientations are likely to be acceptable in Sydney, and major cities, but in more rural areas less so; and in any case privacy of personal and family life is expected. Some Australian agency sources are listed in Appendix 12.

6.9 NEW ZEALAND ORGANISATIONS

New Zealanders are very approachable and have one of the least hierarchical and most open societies, so speak your mind, but they can be reserved regarding family life. They value the rights and opinions of each individual, and New Zealand is making a success of its multicultural society, with whites and Maoris benefiting from the diversity of talents – in the business and sports field. Don't expect much talk during a meal.

6.10 INTERNATIONAL ORGANISATIONS

Many organisations have a head office based somewhere other than in these few areas listed, or have a joint or genuine multinational base. If so, unless you have evidence that they have a particular style, approach them in your own way; you will at least then have the advantage of behaving in the manner that comes most naturally to you.

7
Make the most of your résumé

The purpose of a résumé is to get you an interview. But it also has a life beyond that, so it is doubly important. (There are seven example résumés in Appendices 4 and 5).

Résumés and cvs (cv stands for *curriculum vitae* – life record) are essentially the same, but you can make a distinction. Cvs are more often used in the academic world, and record what you have studied and done. They are more comprehensive and therefore longer – you more or less add experience to a cv as you acquire it. Whereas a résumé has one main purpose in life – it is a carefully designed marketing document presenting the best evidence at this time why someone should employ you. So presentation in a résumé is more important and if you add more experience to a résumé, you may need to edit what is already there to make sure it continues to have high impact.

A well-prepared résumé gives you a huge advantage. Once you have prepared it, you can send it off to as many prospective employers as you like for not much more effort than a new address on your covering letter, and the cost of the postage (you can even email it). You need to update it every year or so, and it usually pays to fine tune at least the covering letter and to some extent the résumé, but provided you have put in the necessary effort to design a good résumé, you should, if you need to, be able to use it for almost any employer.

So what makes a good résumé?

7.1 HOW RECRUITERS SCREEN RÉSUMÉS

How many pages should my résumé be? This is one of the most frequently asked questions. The answer depends on knowing how organisations select who to interview from the résumés they receive. This is often called 'résumé screening' and there are three basic ways of doing it:

1 *Professional*: A person (often from human resources or an agency hired specifically to do this) will go through the résumés, to identify whether candidates have the competencies required. This person must therefore have at least a reasonable idea of what competencies are necessary. The information may come from the manager in whose department the job is located, or from a prior job analysis or job description, or from the advertisement. They may well have a decision sheet which allocates points to various activities and competencies, and those résumés that score above a certain cut-off will go through to interview.

2 *Automatic*: Résumés may be optically scanned and the name, address, qualification, etc information, as well as key words from the competencies described in the résumé, will be automatically loaded onto a database, and a selection made from those résumés that most closely fit the job requirements. These résumés are then available for any subsequent jobs that become vacant within the organisation. This method is particularly likely to be used by American organisations, and for technical/service-related jobs, especially information technology where the organisation receives a large number of résumés.

3 *Gut feel*: Someone (the manager who has the vacancy or HR adviser/recruiter, or someone from a recruitment agency) will look through the résumés and just pick those that look good. A typical advertisement in a national paper may generate in the region of 600 replies, so this means that if the people screening résumés took one minute to look through each, it would take two days, allowing for breaks. Busy screeners in this situation usually glance at a résumé and spend no more than ten seconds deciding whether to read it more carefully or to reject it.

Until quite recently, method 3 was the most used method. This meant that busy people were sifting through often a large number of résumés, and tended to favour fairly short (two-page maximum), eye-catching résumés. So your first half page was doubly important, because that was all the screener had time to read in the first ten seconds before deciding whether to read more, or reject it! However in the past ten years, more organisations, if they have not already moved to online application forms, have begun using methods 1 and 2, especially in the information technology industry.

These methods tend to favour the slightly longer, less terse, more comprehensive résumé, which tries to ensure that **all** the positive evidence you have is included. But be reasonable – anything over four pages (perhaps five pages if you have lots of experience) is going to count against you if a screener is scoring it, and also at interview (since your résumé will usually be the first impression an interviewer has of you, as they look through résumés to prepare for the interview). If nothing else a long, rambling résumé does not bode well for your ability to present important evidence clearly and concisely.

The problem is that you are unlikely to know which method of screening is going to be used. So what do you do?

Length of résumé

First, what a résumé does **not** have to be. It should not be more than four to five pages, and two to three is probably best. On the other hand, don't get so obsessed with keeping it to a certain size that you lose a clear description of what you have done (unless an employer specifies that résumés must be a certain length, in which case you just have to shorten it as best you can). If you really need three pages to describe properly what you have done, leave it at three pages. Two and a half pages looks awkward, and the information on the last half page is usually ignored, so try to shorten it to two, or if you really can't, add more detail to bring it to three. It does not have to be so cleverly designed that just looking at it says clearly that you are a budding graphic artist, with different graphics, fonts, borders and backgrounds. Finally, your résumé should not claim great things that you have done, if you haven't.

7.2 PERSONAL DETAILS

What your résumé **should** contain is a complete account of all your achievements and activities. Whilst you can (and may have to) fine tune it to a particular job or employer, it is as well to start preparing a general résumé that you feel gives the best description of who you are and what you have done that will fit most purposes.

Whilst almost any design of résumé will do, people who look at them expect to find certain information, so it is as well to include this early on.

Name at top

Start with your full name in bold letters at the top. If a selector is looking for your résumé, you may as well make it easy for them to find it. Put your full name, because there may be others with a similar name.

Contact details

Then give contact details, including full mailing address, email and phone, preferably mobile, to give them the best chance to contact you at the first attempt. If you have more than one address (for example if you are studying at university but will be at home during the vacations), give both addresses with dates.

Date of birth

Provide your date of birth (which may be used by some organisations to decide if you are suitable for their position or not, and may also be used to define you as a unique applicant, especially if you have a common name like John Smith). American and some other organisations will have a policy not to consider your age as a criterion, and many of the best organisations from other countries will do so as well. But for a general résumé, unless you feel particularly strongly that you do not want to disclose your age, just provide your date of birth (if you put your age, it will be out of date within 12 months).

7.3 STATEMENT OF OBJECTIVE, OR SUMMARY

American résumés typically place a statement of objective next, for example:

'Objective:

An entry level position in business management that will enable me to use my financial and technical skills in a high achieving team.'

Or, for someone with more experience:

'A Senior Manager position in an internationally recognised professional services firm, which will enable me to demonstrate my ability to provide excellent service to existing clients and to gain new ones, as well as guiding less experienced members of a team.'

This reflects American corporate culture. If you are comfortable with this, include a statement of your objective for this job search, or for your career, but make sure you have worked it through carefully, as if it does not fit what the company is offering, you may fail at the first hurdle. If you are not comfortable with this, then just exclude it, and it will fit neatly into your covering letter anyway.

Probably a better approach is to include a three-to-four-line summary of your résumé, in a hard-hitting style. This may include a statement of objective. Write this summary after you have drafted your résumé, and you may want to fine tune this to fit the organisation you are sending it to. Take time and care over this summary – it may well be all that the person screening your résumé reads, so it needs to include all the reasons why they really must interview you. To keep this within three to four lines you will have to work hard to get just the right wording, but that's not a bad thing to have to do anyway – you may find it helps you to see yourself as you want others to see you.

7.4 SELECTING YOUR BEST EVIDENCE

The next part is the most important – far more important than what format or chronology to use. It requires you to answer the question:

'What is the best evidence I have to persuade the organisations I am applying to that I am one of the best people to interview, and subsequently employ?'

Start with a rough structure, and prepare a first draft – some items are straightforward: exam results, even if not as good as you may wish, are nonetheless a concrete set of achievements, and are important to list. Date order is what selectors usually expect to find, so use this unless you have some compelling reason to do otherwise. Sketch out roughly in date order, starting with the present and going back to what you have done at school. List and describe all your jobs and tasks and responsibilities and achievements. This gives you a backbone to your résumé.

Checklist of what to include

Now, with this on one side, answer the following questions, slotting them into whatever school, university or job they belong to if you haven't already, listing everything that comes to mind first, then prioritising:

Have you any prizes or recommendations – for sport, school, university, work, out-of-school work, community or voluntary work? Have any teams you were part of won or done well in anything? Include contracts or new clients your team gained.	
Have you taken part in any project or team activity, or hobby-based task – like building a computer with others, for example – or a game, or organised a holiday or weekend away or visit to a concert?	
What are the most impressive technical or financial or scientific or people-related projects you have worked on?	
What were the most difficult challenges you had to overcome, and how did you do this?	
When did you have to show leadership, to persuade others (perhaps only one other person) to do something, or to continue with something when they wanted to give up?	
What are your best ideas, perhaps a new way to do something, at work or school or university? How did your idea get put into practice? If not, why not?	
When did you have to work with other people, supporting others, not competing, backing them up – perhaps at work, or outside, or on a project? What effect did your contribution have?	
When did you have to deal with money – perhaps for a team or project – how did you arrange to handle and record it, and was there any occasion when you had to persuade others to have more financial discipline, or identify a new way to save money or make money?	
In which areas do you have technical or financial or other specific competency? Elaborate on this as much as you can, and include expertise gained from previous jobs or university or school courses.	

Have you done anything unusual, or travelled, or played any instrument (even to a basic level)?	
When did you show flexibility and a willingness to do things in a new way?	
When did you have to be thorough and disciplined in what you were doing, and how did you persuade others to be so too?	
What are the most important activities you have been responsible for?	
What languages can you speak or understand, even at a basic level?	
What are the clearest written documents you have produced?	
When did you make your most effective presentation to people, or otherwise persuaded them (perhaps informally) to do something?	
When did you care for anyone, or were sensitive to others needs? Have you taught someone (or more than one)?	
When did you improve the way something is organised? What were the results?	
What other evidence do you think is important if people are to be able to make a proper assessment of your abilities?	

Answering these will not be easy, and don't try to do more than sketch out a few words about each at first, but make sure you know what you are referring to. These questions are encouraging you to cast your net wide, to recognise competencies you may not previously have recognised. Try really hard to have an answer to each of the questions above. It is quite likely that you will be asked something similar to these questions during an interview, so imagine what you would say if asked (after all, you don't know precisely what competencies the organisation thinks are needed for the job). If the interviewer wants to know about a particular competency, it is probably important, so a reply of 'I can't think of any examples' is unlikely to improve your chances – better to have thought about it beforehand when preparing your résumé.

Simple direct action words

People find it much easier to understand what you have done if you use 'I' (rather than 'We' or the passive). Use simple direct words to describe what you did, and include specific quantities and examples. If it genuinely was a team effort, use 'We' and try to specify your particular role.

I	Simple direct action	Specific quantified result

'I organised the team and we reduced costs by 20%.'

'I completed the project within budget and two weeks ahead of schedule.'

'I negotiated to reduce the price we paid by 15%, and achieved this, saving $10,000 a year.'

'We formed a team and diagnosed the fault in the software, corrected it, and I recommended suggestions to prevent it happening again.'

Simple direct action words (examples)

Use these simple direct words to start each activity:

Achieved	Analysed	Built	Completed	Controlled
Delivered	Designed	Diagnosed	Examined	Formed
Helped	Invented	Maintained	Negotiated	Organised
Persuaded	Planned	Prepared	Produced	Recommended
Reduced	Reorganised	Selected	Sold	Solved
Started	Taught	Translated	Won	Wrote

Now add the extra activities that belong to each time section of your life, including for each what you were doing, why, what you achieved, and how, any praise received, any difficulties overcome or to be taken into account.

7.5 EXAGGERATING AND LYING

At this point you will run into the question of exaggeration or even lying. Some studies have indicated that a quarter or more of résumés contain serious errors of fact – what you and I would call lies. Some people might say that if the main purpose of a résumé is to get an interview, then why not lie a bit? If you don't think your résumé as it stands will get you an interview, then why not add an achievement or so, pretend to yourself that you passed that exam, or got a better grade or achieved that recognition or whatever?

But this overlooks four points:

1 You will have to defend the résumé at interview – if it does get you an interview – and if it doesn't then it is a waste of time lying anyway.

2 The employer will probably check some parts of the résumé if they offer you a job. (They are unlikely to do so in many cases before they offer a job, because (a) it is too time-consuming to do this for all the people they interview; and (b) often the checking involves approaching people whom you may not want to know that you have applied for another job – like your present boss for example.) But when they do check, you will almost certainly be in trouble, and may find yourself blacklisted in future or even gaining a reputation for lying.

3 You will not know for sure what aspects, if any, to exaggerate – your résumé, if well presented and including the best evidence you have, may well get you an interview without exaggerating or lying.

4 If you have a résumé that contains only the truth, you can go into an interview with much more confidence than if you are dishonest. And that confidence will stand you in better stead than an exaggeration or lie which will probably be exposed eventually anyway.

The last point is important. Most interviewers now are trained, and even those who are not are usually clever enough to probe areas that seem unlikely or, if they are important, to ask for confirmation, or to check you have the knowledge or skill you claim. If you **know** that your answers are the truth you can be really confident. After all, no matter how good other candidates are, the organisation selected you for interview, and your résumé will stand up against all probing. If you tell the truth you can relax, enjoy the interview and probably get the job. If you lie, you will have to remember which lie, when, and struggle to invent the detail you will need as the interview progresses.

Perspective

This does not mean that you have to downplay your achievements. You should present your achievements in their best light, and you can certainly put a positive gloss on them. The key here is often 'perspective'. For example, there is usually no need to add perspective that reduces any achievements, whereas it is worth including perspective that adds to the achievement. As an illustration:

'Came fourth in projects completed.' No need to mention that there were only five teams involved (but be ready for an observant interviewer to ask this).

'Came fourth in projects completed, out of a total of 150 other teams competing, and we came within 0.5% of coming first.'

The extra perspective adds enormously to the strength of the evidence, and is completely accurate – it should not be seen as bragging, just presenting evidence in the best light.

7.6 JOB-BASED OR COMPETENCY-BASED RÉSUMÉ?

Having arrived at a rough draft, now decide on a number of style and structure points. The most important is whether to organise your résumé by employment and in date order; or in groups of competencies.

1 Jobs and activities you have done, in date order, describing each job or activity with its competencies and achievements; or

2 Competencies, ie grouping the competencies you have, then describing the jobs or activities you acquired them in; or

3 Describing your competencies with minimal reference to the jobs.

In both 2 and 3 you need to list your job history, but it can be brief and at the end of the résumé. In Appendices 5a and 5b there is an example of the same résumé formatted in job order (5a) and in a competency format (5b).

Unless you have a pressing reason to use 2 or 3, I would suggest you use option 1. It is the format most often used, it is straightforward, and is probably the easiest to read, so it provides the information the person screening the résumé needs to make a decision quickly. Reasons for using formats 2 or 3 may include a long period of absence, working for what you consider to be too many employers (which may give rise to suspicion of 'job-hopping'); working for just one or two employers for a long time (if you consider that a problem); or a deliberate (or forced) change of career direction, where you want to emphasise your competencies rather than specific jobs you have done. In all of these you may want to try to change the perspective of the screener.

However, this may be better accomplished by careful choice of words in a chronological résumé; for example, by grouping a number of jobs under a more general description. The functional or competency-based résumé may make the screener spend more time, and he/she may then start to realise your true worth; but it may also make them decide in that first ten seconds that other, clearer résumés are better.

7.7 OTHER STYLE AND FORMAT ISSUES

- Do you list your activities and achievements in strict date order just as they occurred? Or do you separate out education, work and other activities? Probably the best approach is to separate education from work: education then work, then other activities and references at the end, in reverse date order for each category (most recent first), but you can do it differently provided it is consistent and easily understood. Work first, then education may be better if your work achievements are more eye-catching.
- How do you refer to yourself in the résumé? Do you use 'I', or your name ('Smith achieved ...') or do you use the passive ('The following projects were completed ...')? As already described, the best approach is probably the simplest and

most natural – if you were describing what you had done to a friend, you would use 'I'. So use it here: 'I put together a team to reduce our costs of distribution, and within six months we achieved a 10% reduction in costs ...' Note the use of 'I' and 'we' which probably accurately reflects what happened, is not boasting, and can be defended.

- How much detail do you include for your current and previous work? Within the constraints of length (two to three pages for example, a bit longer if you have significant work experience) the answer is: 'As much detail as possible'. Try to make your résumé come alive by explaining what you were (are) responsible for, what are the challenges, what resources you have (don't have) and what you have achieved. Include perspective and dates if they are positive for you.

  Your résumé is a marketing document, so it needs to leap off the page; pretend that you are explaining to a friend your work and its challenges, get excited. Use a simple direct action verb to start each competency, then the problem or task involved, and finally the result or what you achieved. Try particularly to include evidence of achievement, leadership, clear analysis, teamwork, business sense and financial accountability, plus any specific technical or financial or interpersonal competencies relevant for the jobs you are applying for.

- What do you do when you have a year's additional experience and your résumé goes over into a third page? Probably, as you have more evidence, you can start to shorten one or more of the earlier entries, for example school or university experience. Try to find a shorter, more direct way to describe what you did, and be prepared to expand on this if asked at interview. A shorter entry is actually more effective than a longer, rambling one.

- What do you do if you have a gap that you would rather not emphasise? For example, if you were ill and would rather not discuss this, or were out of work, or resting for a time? The easiest option is to include only the dates for all the other activities and hope that an alert interviewer does not notice. Or use less specific dates: for example, instead of 'April 2003–August 2004 Team Leader; November 2004–date Senior Associate', you could put: '2003–4 Team Leader; 2004–date Senior Associate'. The gap is glossed over. After all, most selectors deciding who to interview look for the positive, and if they are considering whether to interview you, they will probably give you the benefit of the doubt on this one, especially since they can't easily contact you to ask for an explanation or for more information. In any case, precise start and finish dates are often blurred, for example, by holiday you take at the end, and times when you start a job in the middle of a month or year.

But be aware that if they check or ask you to confirm precise dates your massaging may become apparent, and you should be prepared to tell the truth if asked a direct question. If you have a criminal conviction there are rules for when you need to disclose this. Usually, after a period of time has elapsed, you are no longer required to disclose it – but there are exceptions.

- Do you provide references and, if so, who? References add weight to a résumé – after all, everything that has gone before is your word alone, whereas if other people are prepared to act as referees for you, then clearly you have had some positive impact on them. Choose two people with whom you have got on well, and who you think would recommend you. They should have some logical relationship to your career – two friends may offer to act as referees, but if they have nothing to do with your work, this is unlikely to be convincing. Whereas your previous two bosses, or previous boss and a mentor or tutor with whom you have had a lot of contact, would be good. Try to confine referees to people who have known you well in the last three to four years. Give the relationship you have with them if it is not apparent, eg previous supervisor, university tutor etc. Or you can put 'References available on request'.

- Trouble with your current boss? If you are having a troubled relationship with your current boss (this may be why you are looking for another job), but have an excellent relationship with another division manager, by all means put this other person down as a referee instead of your current boss, making sure that you tell the truth about his or her correct role (eg Divisional Manager of Distribution). In any case, don't at interview be overly critical of your current boss. It very seldom impresses the interviewer, who is likely to regard it as being disloyal, and who after all may be your next boss if they hire you.

- Won't your present employer resent being asked for references? Generally, employers will not take up references until they are about to make a job offer – particularly if you are already employed and one of your referees is your current boss. So it is perfectly OK to indicate that referees should not be approached without your permission. With this exception, you should only name a person on your résumé if you have asked for and received their permission; and it is best to brief them in at least general terms on what sort of work you are looking for, and what you would like them to say. It confuses the issue, and may even cost you the job, if your referee recommends you highly and says that your ambition has always been to be an accountant, if you have changed your mind and have applied to be a lawyer instead. So make sure your tutor/referee knows what you want, and what you would like her or him to say. It may be worth contacting them promtly, in case the organisation takes up references earlier than expected.
- Should you prepare a new résumé for each organisation you apply to, angling each one towards the particular qualities you think they are looking for? The answer to this is yes, in an ideal world, but in practice a standard résumé will probably do, provided you have taken care in preparing it in the first place. You may be able to write an extra paragraph or two to add weight in specific areas you know a particular organisation is keen on, but more than this is probably not worth it. If there are particular areas you want to emphasise, it may be easier to include this in your covering letter (see next chapter). In any case, most organisations that are especially keen on particular evidence ask for this direct in an online or paper application form. If they don't, your standard résumé should be fine.

- Should you include a photo? A few organisations ask you to include a photo. If so, obviously include one – and a good one at that. It is unfortunate but true that when volunteers were asked to rate how trustworthy people were just by looking at their photographs, they tended to conclude that those with the most attractive photographs were also the most trustworthy. So it is well worth making sure that if you do include a photograph, it is a good, flattering one.

  It does not have to be costly. You may well have a photo already taken by a photographer or friend; or you may ask a friend with a digital camera to take a large number of photographs from a range of angles in different lights, using a variety of zooms and distance (zoom taken from a bit further away may be better than wide angle from closer). Delete most of them, pick the best three or four, modify them as much as you want (eg for colour, or pink eye), print them, and pick the best. If you do not have to include a photo, it genuinely is up to you. When screening résumés, most professionals focus on just the key competencies, which is as it should be – not having a photo will not hurt your chances at all. However, if you have an attractive photo, it may just be enough to catch their perhaps slightly jaded attention, and get you onto the interview list.

- Do you include all your school or university results or only a summary, if at all? This depends on what else you have to include in your résumé. If you don't have much work experience, then an employer will be interested in what other evidence you do have – in this case specific exam results (if positive) are worth including, especially languages, sciences and maths. Remember the three screening methods described earlier in Section 7.1. If you think your résumé may be screened optically I would suggest that you do not reduce it. On the other hand, if you have more than a few years' work experience, you can start to reduce the space given to school, and just present a summary of the best results, eg '10 GCSEs including A* in French and Art'.

Always include any languages, and any relevant exam subjects, eg information technology. However, no need to specify the F for geography, for example. University degrees of 2:2 or above are worth specifying, as are any prizes and awards or distinctions; otherwise just put 'BSc Biology' or whatever. Employers often look only at the highest degree, so if you do not feel that your first degree does you justice, getting a Master's will enable you to distract attention from it. Be aware that university degrees and professional qualifications are pieces of evidence that most employers will check – sometimes by asking to see the original certificate, sometimes by contacting the university.

- What do you do if some of your educational achievements were gained abroad, and are in a different format from that of the country in which you are applying? In this case you need to explain briefly enough context to give your educational achievement meaning. For example, 'Attended … University in Belgium, achieved 83% Grande Distinction (in the top quartile of results, equivalent to a 2:1 in the UK). Sometimes, if you can find a quote from *The Times Educational Supplement* or other respected reference this is very helpful, for example, 'International Baccalaureate 38/45 (*The Times Educational Supplement* rates this as equivalent to AABB at A level)'. The following table from the J P Morgan website can be used as a guide to some equivalencies:

1st Degree level	UK	GERMANY	FRANCE	ITALY	SPAIN	NETHERLANDS	BELGIUM	TURKEY
Equivalencies	2:1	1 – 2.5	12 – 20	85–110	7–10	7–10	Minimum 80%–Grande distinction	2.5

The US equivalent is Grade Point Average (GPA). In principle a GPA of more than about 3.4 (out of 4) would count as equivalent to a 2:1 in the UK (and hence equivalent to the grades from the other countries listed in the table). However, far more important is the university awarding the degree. So a GPA of 3.4 from Harvard or MIT, for instance, is far more competitive than a 3.4 from some other universities. Some US employers consult reference books which list the ratio of the university's applicants to those admitted, in order to gain some idea of how competitive a university is.

- What do you do if you don't have much, if any, work experience? First, if you can, try to get some, even one week's work as a temporary will be worth mentioning. And second, you must have been doing something; you should still be able to think of evidence from school, university, friends, holidays, gap year etc when you were faced with a challenge, and showed qualities such as teamwork, leadership, clear thinking etc. Describe this with sufficient detail so that someone unfamiliar with your situation will understand what you did and why it is useful evidence.

7.8 SHOW YOUR DRAFT RÉSUMÉ TO A FRIEND

Now show your draft résumé to a friend, parent, adviser, tutor, colleague, anyone who will spend five minutes looking through it and tell you what is unclear or muddled or needs expanding. Don't expect them to check your facts, but they should be able to tell you if you have used jargon that is not obvious, been unclear in your dates, or insufficiently described what you actually did in a particular role.

Finally, and particularly if you believe that your résumé will have to stand out from hundreds of others being screened by for example a recruitment or other agency, try to prepare a format or layout or photo that makes your résumé strikingly different, yet professional. Otherwise, a clear format that tells the facts will be sufficient – an over-exotic format may even muddy the clarity you have created.

7.9 FORMAT HINTS FOR RÉSUMÉS THAT ARE LIKELY TO BE SCANNED

If your résumé is likely to be optically scanned – particularly if you are applying for jobs in the information technology area – there are some ways you can help to ensure your résumé is accurately scanned:

- Put each telephone number on a separate line.
- Use basic fonts so that each character is separate from the next, and keep *italics* and <u>underline</u> to a minimum. Use CAPITALS and **bold** to emphasise points.
- Don't use boxes or tables or graphics, and left justify your text – not centre.

Scanning requires each page to be separated – so don't use staples (paper clips are OK). It is not unknown for résumé pages to be disordered, or for a page 2 on the reverse of page 1 to be missed when they are scanned, so consider sending a two- or three-page résumé on separate sheets rather than back to back, and/or number your pages '1 of 3', '2 of 3', '3 of 3' so that if this does happen they may still be scanned in the correct order, or if not, then the recruiter will be able to re-order them.

Add detail to jobs you have done, and to the descriptions of what your responsibilities were. For example, don't just put 'Assistant'. Put 'Sales Assistant in the Digital Camera Team', and go on to describe in some detail all the skills you had to use to help customers to decide which digital camera to purchase. Remember – because scanners don't get tired, you can put in a bit more detail, and page 2 is likely to be scanned just as efficiently as page 1.

Use high-quality paper, and a good-quality printer – go to a print shop or borrow a friend's printer if necessary – and send your résumé in a full-size envelope so you don't need to fold it.

7.10 FORMAT HINTS FOR RÉSUMÉS TO BE EMAILED

This is very different from online application forms – and much quicker, because you choose the format and the information. But if the person receiving your cover email and résumé can't open your attachment, you have a problem – and they won't take much time trying to open it.

Five years ago the safest approach was to save your résumé as a text-only file when you 'save' or 'save as'. The disdvantage of this is that almost the only way to emphasise anything is by using CAPITALS. Bold, italics etc just become plain text. Use the space bar instead of tabs, and do spell checks before you save – there won't be one after. Don't use symbols – they probably won't appear, or will be confusingly transformed into something different. Check your résumé in its new text-only format before you send it.

These days though the standard 'basic' format is Word 2000. Every firm should be able to open this, and it allows you to retain the formatting. So I would use Word 2000 and, only if that fails, switch to text only.

8
Covering letters and applying to less well-known organisations

A covering letter with a résumé (perhaps sent by email or cut and pasted into the 'Contact us' or recruitment section of an organisation's website) is the easiest and most efficient way for you to apply to organisations. Unfortunately, as indicated in the previous chapter, companies may well have decided on the information they want in order to make a well-judged selection, and require you to complete an online application or application form. See the next chapter for advice on this. However, if you can send a covering letter and résumé, you can apply to 20 organisations in little more time than it takes to change the name of the organisation you are writing to, write the address on 20 envelopes and post them.

Of course, if you are only applying for one or two very specific positions, then you can craft your covering letter with more care.

A covering letter can take many forms, but a good guide is to position the name of the organisation you are applying to at the top left-hand side. If the covering letter is to an organisation that has a reputation for being formal, or it is a high priority for you, then include their address in the covering letter and use normal letter conventions. But if you need to save time, many organisations will not penalise you for leaving it out when they screen your application. Include the specific name of the person you are applying to, as well as the job you are applying for, or a reference if you have it, or at least write 'Attention: Recruitment' or something similar. You need your covering letter to get to the right place. Put your own contact address including postcode, phone and email at the top right-hand side, a title for the letter in capitals or underlined (for example, APPLICATION FOR ACCOUNT EXECUTIVE), and then three main paragraphs, as follows.

8.1 COVERING LETTER FORMAT

Paragraph 1

In the first paragraph, repeat the position you are applying for, and explain what prompted you to apply – for example, whether you saw their advertisement in a newspaper, or a friend already in their organisation suggested you apply. Mention that you are enclosing your résumé, so that it stays with your letter.

Paragraph 2

The second paragraph is the most important part of your letter. Explain why you believe that your résumé fits you for the requirements of the job, and emphasise any parts that you think are particularly important and relevant. For example, you may already have worked there on a temporary basis; or perhaps a friend who already works with them recommended that you apply, etc. This is your real chance to fine tune your application and to sound excited about the specific organisation you are applying to, so add some detail if you can.

Paragraph 3

In the final paragraph, explain how keen you are to be considered for the job, and that you hope they will give you the opportunity to explain this further at interview. You would be pleased to attend an interview at any suitable time (and note here any dates you definitely cannot make). If you are applying to an agency where you do not know the client they represent, make clear any organisations you do **not** want your résumé sent to (eg your current organisation). In any case you would appreciate a response by email/phone/address (indicate which you prefer) before (and give a date two to three weeks away).

A frequent but annoying problem is how to start the letter. If you know the name of the person you are applying to, this is easy: 'Dear Ms Jones', or whatever. But if you do not know a specific name? 'Dear Sir/Madam', or 'To whom it may concern' sounds remote, 'Dear Recruiter' sounds desperate. Sometimes the best approach is to leave this out altogether, and just put 'Attention: Recruitment' in the address. Your letter will stand quite well without it, and there is no need to call anyone 'Dear' if you do not even know who they are. Much better of course is to find the name of the person to apply to if you can. You can see an example cover letter in Appendix 4f.

You may not get a response within your time-frame, but it is reasonable to ask for one, and most professional firms will aim to respond within what they consider a proper time. However, be aware that some firms may specify or have a policy that they do not reply to unsolicited applications, and advertisements may say that only candidates invited to interview will be contacted – some organisations will not even have the courtesy to put this in the advertisement.

8.2 BY-PASSING RECRUITMENT DEPARTMENTS

Many organisations have in place a recruitment department or agency to screen applications. Sometimes you may want to try to by-pass it. This usually depends on you doing your homework well enough to know who is actually doing the recruiting (for instance, the supervisor of the department that has the vacant position). Ideally you need to get your résumé to them before they have even started the formal process, or at least have a friend to give you a recommendation.

Your friends and colleagues are an especially rich source of employment possibilities. As well as giving you inside information on what it is like to work in their organisation, or location, or type of job, they can also recommend you for positions. Many firms, particularly American-based ones, have schemes which provide incentives to staff who recommend people they know who are subsequently recruited. So you may really be in a win-win situation here.

Be prepared to follow up if you have not received a reply within your time-frame, but don't expect a large volume of positive responses. If they are not interested in you, it may be that you are better chasing other organisations.

8.3 IF YOU HAVE APPLIED BEFORE

Companies often keep records of people who have applied to them, or who have attended an interview or assessment centre. If they have seen you or your résumé within the past year, they often conclude that if they didn't choose you last time, there is no reason to change their mind within one year. After a year though, there may be new evidence, so they look more carefully.

8.4 GIVE YOURSELF A BETTER CHANCE – APPLY FOR LESS WELL-KNOWN ORGANISATIONS

Organisations with easily recognised names like big banks, oil companies, retail stores, pharmaceutical companies, get lots and lots of applicants, literally hundreds for every vacancy they have, so they are spoiled for choice because the applicants are either too lazy or haven't the experience to think of other organisations. On the other hand, less well-known organisations often receive very few applications, and are therefore likely to give greater consideration to the applicants who do apply. So you may well find that it is worth thinking of these.

Follow up likely leads

Your past experience has probably given you some idea of the organisations that may be right for you. Have you applied to that smaller bank, or that local company which is highly thought of, or even that rapidly growing organisation that you read about yesterday, or the firm that your friend is already working for? No need to lower your standards, very often the smaller organisations are faster growing and more successful by many criteria than a large number of household names.

Anywhere you have worked, even for a vacation job or as a temporary, is worth considering, especially if you can genuinely say you enjoyed working there. Your experience there will stand you in good stead even though you are probably applying for a much more demanding role. It's certainly worth following up such leads at slow times when you have few other applications in the pipeline. Alternatively, web search, and/or what is sometimes better, a chat with your friends may well identify good organisations to apply to. Even if friends' companies do not have a referral or employee recommendation incentive scheme, their suggestions could be more fruitful than you imagine.

Google or Yahoo or other web searches can be particularly good. Just enter the job or activities you are interested in, or even the well-known organisations you have heard of, and see what else comes out. Or try one or more recruitment agencies either in person or via the web. Less well-known organisations are likely to be just as keen to attract good talent, but recognise that their name or brand is not well known, so they may retain an agency to help them. The agency will have everything to gain by proposing you to their client(s) whose needs fit your qualities and experience. The added advantage is that if it all works, the agency will keep in touch with you, for when you are ready for another move …

9
Online applications – how to apply effectively in least time

You may as well recognise that online applications are annoying because you have to present much the same information each time, but in subtly different ways to fit with the precise questions asked. Be prepared to spend about two hours per online application, although as you get more used to them, you will find you can get faster than this. So it's as well to start them early, and do them in a batch – as many as you can do in a weekend for example. Online applications are especially likely for new graduate applicants.

9.1 YOUR RÉSUMÉ AND CUT AND PASTE

The key to online applications is your résumé, and the cut and paste function, plus a little bit of discipline to save your answers to previous online applications, so you don't have to develop the answers to the same questions twice or even more times. A few firms allow you to include your résumé in addition to answering their questions. You will not know how much attention they will pay to your résumé though, and will probably have to answer the questions, even though much of the information is already in your résumé.

If you are working from your own computer, this part is going to be easier, but you can also work from a friend's computer or from an internet café or library, that will allow you to upload a CD or other storage with your résumé and other answers. Be careful about applying from work – organisations usually have rules about employees' personal use of PCs, and applying to other firms generally fits this category.

Check what's involved early

Start by looking at three or four online applications – many can be looked at without having to input your name and address, but if this is not possible, you may be able to save just your name and address, having looked at the questions, and come back to them later. In the worst case you could always consider making up a name and address in order to see the rest of the questions. You do not want to make an application with only your actual name and address entered, because the system will then reject you. When you later come to apply for real, you will be rejected again automatically, because as already indicated, organisations usually check to see if you have applied before. If so, and your previous application was made within the past year, they will just give you the same decision they gave you before, because you are unlikely to have significant new information to add.

When you have your three or four online applications, you will probably see that they are pretty similar, especially if you are applying for similar organisations and jobs. Now look at your résumé. You will most likely see that it provides answers to many of the questions asked by the online applications, with a bit of tweaking and changing. For example, you will probably find that after the obvious sections dealing with name, address and other factual information like educational achievements (which will take some time to input, even using cut and paste where you can – which is not easy), most of the questions are of the 'Give an example when you showed [some particular quality or character]' variety. For example: 'Give an example when you showed leadership', or 'Give an example when you showed teamwork', or 'Give an example when you had to overcome a particularly difficult problem'.

9.2 TRANSFORMING YOUR RÉSUMÉ INTO THE ONLINE APPLICATION

Your résumé gives the best picture and evidence of you that you can provide. So you want to get as much of what is in your résumé as you can into your online application. Look carefully at the questions in the online application. You will probably find that a section of your résumé pretty much answers one of the questions. For example, the best answer to the question of when you showed teamwork is that part of your résumé when you were working with a team to tackle a particular problem or challenge.

So cut and paste that part of your résumé into the online application, then read it and the precise questions they asked again to make sure your answer makes sense, and edit it quickly to improve it if you think it needs it. Now move on to the next question. You will probably find another part of your résumé fits this question, perhaps not quite as exactly but 90%. So cut and paste that, and then do the necessary editing and continue in this way.

You may find that it is easier to edit your answer in your own format before pasting it to their application, rather than pasting then editing in the online application format, if only because the edit functions in online applications are often pretty basic. Do not use the same example to answer more than one question, tempting though it may be.

At some point you will find a question that really has no answer in your résumé. There is no alternative here – you will have to answer it. Work out the best example you can, and then save it for future use.

When you have done this you will find that you have prepared as you are doing it, an almost perfect Interview Preparation Table (See 10.3 and Appendix 6) which will immeasurably improve your performance in the interview. So the time spent is doubly valuable.

Aim to finish your Plan A online applications in a weekend

If your cut and pastes are working well, you should have almost finished all your Plan A applications (ie your most favoured ones) in one weekend while you have time and it's all fresh in your mind (it's easier to cut and paste when you are familiar with everything). In any case, you will probably get some very quick replies to some of these applications, and you don't want to have some Plan A interviews which you may prefer coming much later, when you are under pressure to decide whether to accept an offer from one of the early bird organisations.

Plan B and Plan C applications

You should also aim to complete as well, at least those Plan B and Plan C applications that have deadlines that you will miss if you wait before replying for responses to Plan A applications. These former are your insurance policy. As discussed in Chapter 10 on interviews, you are also much more likely to perform well at interview with your top-rated organisations if you already have at least one other interview with another organisation – better still, a job offer – even if it is from an organisation that is not top of your list. It will give you confidence, and so you have everything to gain by progressing some Plan B and Plan C applications early as well.

10
Interviews

There are lots of examples in business where someone with an apparently better product loses out to a rival who can present their case better. That's why lawyers are often successful in business – some use the law, but the ones who do really well earn their money by presenting a case, and presenting it well.

In trading, government, the professions, banking, or almost any business, the same applies – you may have a product or policy or technique that is undervalued, and then work to persuade others of its real merits. In this case the product is **you**.

Of course, good presentation does *not* mean that it is not necessary to have a good product. It's just that even the best also needs to be presented well.

When you are selected for interview, you know that you have already got what the selectors regard as the required competencies, good experience and a suitable approach. You need to assess again what evidence you want, to make sure you present them in your answers. At the same time you must be quick enough to respond to any unexpected questions, **smile** and present a confident, relaxed approach.

New graduates

Most financial organisations in the UK interview prospective graduates during the October to December term, and hold assessment centres often from November to January, so be prepared for early interviews. Many non-financial organisations interview for their graduate entry from January to March, so their deadlines for applications are later, as are their interviews. Other countries and other entry streams will have different deadlines and interview timings, so it's important to be clear on what these are. If you are going to be out of the country during this time, write, phone or email early and most organisations will find a way to fit you in, if they think you are good enough.

Experienced staff

Interviews for experienced staff can take place at any time, so you will have to try to arrange how to get there without alerting your current employer. In any case, it is always worth asking whether interviews can take place close to where you are and/or at a time that suits you. Don't be too dogmatic about this, but there is usually some flexibility in interview schedules, particularly if you applied early.

If the interviews are some way from home, you may get paid expenses, so have a short break on the company! If your current employer doesn't know you are applying for other positions, you may have to work out various ways to find time to attend interviews. Before or after work; on the way to or from some other meeting or airport; lunch; all these are common tactics. Some can become over-used – five or six dentist appointments in a short period may attract more than concern about your teeth!

Culture

Different cultures will interview in often quite different ways, sometimes driven by the conventions and labour laws in the country of their head office as well as the labour laws and conventions of the country in which you are applying. So bear this in mind when you are going to the interview, and you should perform better than others who have not given this much thought. See Chapter 6 for more detail.

10.1 HOW INTERVIEWERS DECIDE WHO TO SELECT

There is some pretty compelling evidence that unstructured interviews (ie interviews where the interviewer simply asks whatever questions come into their head at the time, without having any structure to make sure they cover all the evidence they need to collect) are almost **useless**. Sorry to use such emphatic wording, but all the evidence is that interviews that don't follow some sort of structure are far more likely simply to reinforce all the existing prejudices of the interviewer.

In these circumstances the chances of successfully filling the vacancy would be almost as good if the interviewer simply put the résumés of the people he or she had to interview on the floor of their office, and threw a coin over their shoulder until it landed on one, then hired that person. See Appendix 3 for a rigorous analysis by Professor Neil Anderson and Dr Nicole Cunningham-Snell of the accuracy of various methods of selection.

The well-structured interview – a co-operative discussion

Most organisations are aware of this by now, so you may expect at least a reasonably professional structured interview, that will be based on the competencies or requirements of the job and any future development the organisation has in mind. (What is a competence? See 3.2.) Questions will often be aimed at seeking evidence for particular competencies or experiences that are important for the job. The interviewer will probably have some type of interview form, which they will complete during the interview or immediately after. This form will help guide them to ask about all the evidence they need. So you as the candidate should come prepared to do everything you can to help the interviewer to find this. Put this way, the interview becomes a co-operative discussion, with a potential win-win outcome, rather than any test or exam or win-lose outcome.

If the interviewer is writing, they are unlikely to be able to listen also to what you are saying, so be prepared to pause until they have finished and re-established eye contact with you. If they ask you to continue while they write, you may have to do this, but be aware that they are unlikely to take in more than half of what you say!

Focus on the competencies required

In summary, most professional interviewers (who may be managers, HR advisers or recruiters or recruitment agency staff) will have a reasonably good idea of what competencies are important for the job or career you are applying for, and will rate you on the evidence you present for each competency. If you are applying for a technical or scientific position, don't be surprised to be asked a number of questions dealing with business or people issues. This is because the organisation wants to find out whether you have the potential to become a manager in future.

Sometimes all the competencies are regarded as equally important, sometimes a few are regarded as very important, even crucial, and are given more weight. Sometimes the decision on who to employ or pass to the next stage of selection is made by adding together the ratings for each competency (suitably weighted) and after a brief consideration deciding on the candidate with the highest rating. At other times, the interviewer may be guided by the competencies, but decide in a more holistic way, without allocating numbers. The unstructured interviewer may often decide within the first five minutes on the basis of whatever they like in that time, and spend the rest of the time looking for evidence to confirm their original decision.

10.2 WHAT YOU ARE AIMING TO ACHIEVE IN THE INTERVIEW

At the interview you are going to concentrate on presenting what really matters – your achievements, and examples illustrating the various qualities and behaviours the organisation is looking for. Preparing your résumé will have helped you to select the most impressive examples and present them in the best possible light.

The huge advantage you now have is that if you have followed the advice in Chapter 7 on preparing a résumé, and Chapter 9 (online applications), the answers you submitted to secure the interview are all true. You should have complete confidence in them. Other people may have lied a bit, or exaggerated, and will be stressed, anticipating probing questions that will reveal this. But your answers are simply the truth presented properly, with just sufficient stretching to make sure you get the credit you deserve, but not so much that an interviewer could take exception to it. They will expect some perspective to be added to the evidence anyway.

You should be able to cope with any amount of probing on those answers (because the interviewers probably will probe a bit) whilst at the same time putting forward additional evidence you want them to be aware of that was not in your application. (For example, emphasise activities that you may have used for other online applications, or pieces of your résumé that didn't fit into their online application, if that's how you applied to them. It's probably worth bringing along one or two copies of your résumé, and maybe even highlighting for yourself these extra bits of information.)

The best predictors of future job performance

Most properly trained interviewers will use some variant of behavioural or competency-based interviewing. This relies on the principle that:

The best predictor of future behaviour and job perfomance is past behaviour.

Or in other words, if the interviewer has identified the competencies or requirements needed for good or very good performance in the job, he or she needs to collect from you evidence about when you have shown (or not shown) similar behaviours in similar circumstances. So, to take a very simple example, if the job involves selling products or services to new clients, it will probably involve a significant amount of (a) gaining a good relationship with new people quickly; (b) getting to know their requirements; and (c) persuading them that your product or service meets their needs better than any other alternative.

Therefore, the interviewer will ask for examples of when you have done this in the past. Now you may not have done any selling before, but this is the strength of competency-based interviewing, because by breaking down the job into discrete competencies, it allows you to identify occasions in different jobs or even university or leisure activities when you had to exhibit each of the three competencies identified.

So you may have had to gain a good relationship with new people quickly when you were working in a ski chalet or as a tour guide. You may have had to find out people's requirements when you were doing a survey as part of your university course or for a local council which involved finding out what people wanted from the public transport system in your city. And you may have had to persuade people to come on a group tour that you were organising for the mountaineering or diving club in your home town. So you actually do have quite reasonable evidence of competency in each of the three key areas, although you have never actually had a selling job.

Using competencies to your advantage

This is why you should welcome a properly structured interview – it gives you a much better chance to demonstrate how good you are, even if you don't have exactly the experience that an untrained interviewer might think is needed. **But it is up to you to think widely enough to give the best evidence you can of the**

competency the interviewer asks you about. Don't be afraid to request clarification of the competency. So if they want you to give them an example of when you had to defuse a difficult situation, ask them to elaborate a bit on what they mean. This will give you time and quite possibly a much better lead on what they are looking for, and will enable you to give a really good example. By all means give an example from your résumé if it is relevant – after all, your résumé got you the interview, so they must think the evidence in it is pretty good, and they may be keen to probe you on that evidence to check that it all really happened just as you said in the résumé.

So expect lots of questions along the lines of 'Can you give me an example of when you ... [had to show leadership, or teamwork, or integrity, or customer orientation or imagination, for example]?' Your answers should in most cases, come straight from your résumé; where they don't, you will at least have had practice in identifying these examples for other competencies.

10.3 INTERVIEW PREPARATION TABLE

Would you like a simple technique that will really improve your performance at interview? You need to prepare a table along the lines of the example in Appendix 6 – this can dramatically improve your performance and confidence to the extent that you will almost end up conducting the interview yourself. In the left-hand column list the competencies or qualities you expect the interviewers to ask about. Then identify in the second column the best evidence from your résumé for each, and note this in just a few points, enough to enable you to remember the activity. If you have already used your best example for another question, include it in the second column, but also think of what your next best example would be, and put this in note form in the third column against the relevant question. If you have already used this elsewhere, include it, but think of what the next best evidence is, and put this in the fourth column. You won't need more than four columns.

You will find that this table can be used for most organisations, and the more you use it the better you will get. Feel free to print it out and have it with you at interview – after all, most business people will empathise with someone who has taken the trouble to prepare, and anyway they will probably think you are just referring to your résumé, which in a way you are. But after a few times you won't need the paper version.

10.4 TYPICAL EXAMPLE INTERVIEW QUESTIONS

In addition to preparing for the usual 'Give me an example of a time when you showed leadership/analysis/motivation/team-work/working under pressure' sort of questions, it's also worth just practising in your head or with rough notes the answers you would give to some of the more common general interview questions, such as:

How did you get here today? Isn't it awful weather? Did you watch the news/sport last night? Don't get worried by these – the interviewer is almost certainly not testing your general knowledge. He or she is trying to help you both to relax and get to know each other by initiating some general conversation that will not form part of the formal interview. Treat it as such and respond warmly. There just may be a follow-on question relating to the news for example, but it should flow naturally.

Why did you choose to apply to us? Describe how you found this organisation, how you think you can contribute, and what you want to achieve – for example, development.

How would you describe our business/main competitors? Try to be comprehensive, if they want you to go into lots of detail, they will ask you. Personal experience with the product may be relevant but be sparing with it – using BP petroleum is not a very good reason for wanting to join BP, nor does it add much to a description of BP for example. You really need to have at least looked at their website, and put their name into a search engine, and checked anything recent in *The Economist* or similar magazine.

What are our main competitive advantages/the main challenges facing our business? Where should we be in five to ten years' time? If you are genuinely interested in joining them, you should have thought about this, and reading *The Economist* or information from web searches should give you a reasonable answer.

Why do you want to be a trader/engineer/systems designer/project manager/analyst/partner/director/consultant/banker/lawyer/accountant? Describe briefly how you came to choose this particular career/job. Concentrate on what you enjoy doing, and your strengths. If you followed Chapter 2 on career choice this will give you a huge advantage here.

What do you want to be doing in five to ten years' time? You may want to be doing the same job but in greater professional depth, or at a more senior level, or have progressed and broadened to be responsible for a wider set of activities, or to have switched into a related but growing field – you choose.

Tell me about yourself. Either a gentle opening question, or a mark of a lazy interviewer. Either way, briefly summarise your résumé.

What are your main strengths? Describe two or three from your résumé.

What are your main weaknesses? A more difficult question; you need to turn it round to one of your strengths. So something like 'I sometimes carry on trying to improve a product or report even when it already meets the minimum standard required'; or 'I sometimes carry on trying to influence a colleague even when others have given up on her'.

Why should we employ you? This question almost seeks reassurance from you that if they recruit you, the organisation will benefit. So describe briefly how competent you are, and how motivated you will be if they recruit you.

How would you estimate how many firemen are needed in this city? They are not checking you out as a future fire chief – unless you applied for this – they are actually using this as a test of how quickly you can think on your feet, and deal with the unexpected.

The question may even be angled more to your professional skills, but nonetheless will require you to think clearly and confidently. This sort of question is more usually asked at final stage selection, so the best way to approach it is described in 13.5. Essentially you have to break the problem into bits, make estimates of each, then combine them again. So, as a very brief example, estimate what is the maximum time you can allow to get to a fire to have a chance of putting it out, estimate how far a fire-engine can travel in this time, how many fire stations you then need, how many firemen to a truck and trucks to a station; then cross-check by considering the cost of each fire in financial and people terms, how much each fireman costs, what are the other benefits they bring, and do a rough cost-benefit analysis.

Technical or scientific questions. Undergraduates often expect to get lots of these, and are surprised when the interview does not include many. Part of the reason is that firms don't know your university syllabus, so are not confident of what it is reasonable to expect you to know; part is that they reckon that if you are going to get a university degree, then there is little point in testing you on it, since the university will be doing that. But you may be given a practical issue to see how well you can apply your university knowledge in practice – for example, here is a wiring or circuit diagram, what would happen if there is a break at this point?

Who else have you applied to, how far have you got with them, have you any outstanding interviews or offers? This is a tricky question – on the one hand, if you say you have applied to a number of other organisations, and have a number of interviews, assessments, and even job offers outstanding, then the interviewer may feel that you are not really committed to their organisation. On the other hand, if you say you have no other interviews or offers, the interviewer may conclude that if you are not good enough for the competition, you are not good enough for them. The best answer is the truth, but presented in such a way as to suggest that you are considering other organisations and are in communication with them, but at the moment their organisation is your first choice.

What salary do you expect/are you currently receiving? Tell the truth about your current income, but feel free to include all benefits etc if you wish to make it appear higher; for example, if your salary is 30,000, and you received a bonus of 5,000 last year plus other benefits worth 7,000, you may say something like, 'I am on 42K this year.' If the question is what salary do you expect, state your expectation clearly, but if you are prepared to discuss this, then make this clear also. It is probably best not to use the word 'negotiate' here – this spells hassle for the employer, particularly if there are strict limitations on what can be offered.

When can you start? (This does not necessarily mean you have the job – it may just mean that there is a requirement for the successful person to start on a certain date, and they are asking everyone this. If you are keen to get the job, describe when you would like to start, but ask when the organisation would need you to start, and say that you will do everything you can consistent with your remaining commitments to your present employer to manage to meet this).

Have you any questions you want to ask? See 10.5 below.

10.5 QUESTIONS TO ASK THE INTERVIEWER

This last question leads to more anxiety than it need. The truth is that at the end of an interview (which is when it is usually asked), the interviewer has usually gained all the evidence they need to make an assessment, and the 'Have you any questions for me?' is really just being polite, and winding down to the end of the interview. After all, if someone has been throwing questions at you for a long time, it **is** only polite to ask if you have any questions – and it also makes sense to check that there is nothing that is unclear to the candidate or that they genuinely want to ask about. But in these circumstances it is very unlikely to have any effect at all on your rating.

There may be a few exceptions to this – a few interviewers may want to test how much homework or preparation you have done on the organisation, and ask this question ('Have you any questions for me?') early on in the interview. It therefore makes sense to have one or two questions prepared about the organisation – you can develop these when you are doing your research – there must be a few aspects that you are unclear about and can reasonably ask about. Hopefully you are interested in the organisation, and genuinely want to find out a bit more about it.

Questions about terms and conditions

The second type of response to this question deals with how you would be employed: salaries, other terms and conditions, location etc – whatever is important to you. So if there are any issues like this that you are concerned about, especially salary, list these also. It is perfectly OK to have your questions on a sheet of paper that you take out of your pocket – after all, the interviewer usually has a form to remind them of questions to ask and how to rate, so it is reasonable for you to have written down the questions you want to ask.

Once you have asked your first question, you will probably start to get a good indication of whether the interviewer is genuinely interested in what you have asked, or whether this was just a preliminary to winding down the interview, and he or she is not really interested. If the latter, there is not much point in continuing to ask questions if you are not getting much in the way of answers, and don't be surprised if the interviewer calls a halt quickly anyway. But in the few cases when the interviewer genuinely uses this as a tactic to get into a discussion about the organisation it is as well to be prepared.

10.6 PROJECTING AN AIR OF CONFIDENCE

Many people are very concerned about what to wear to an interview, and are desperate to create 'a good first impression' because they have heard that an interviewer often makes up his or her mind within the first two minutes. Whilst there is some truth in this, it is probably your character and confidence and facial expression, rather than what you are wearing, that will have most impact on the interviewer, even in the first few minutes. If spending a lot of time choosing what to wear and getting it just right makes you feel better, then certainly do this. But otherwise, dress in a way that you feel comfortable and confident in – 'smart casual', or if you prefer, a business suit – clean and well presented; but do not expect your clothes or your hair style to get you the job.

Why you should smile

Spend more time going over your résumé or the evidence you have presented, and being clear what evidence you want to make sure the interviewer understands. And **smile**. There is no better way to give a good first impression, and it will naturally give you confidence as well. Studies have indicated that people (and interviewers are people too) pay most attention to another's person's eyes and facial expression during the first two minutes of meeting them – and indeed subsequently. Smiling and looking at the interviewer will not only project an air of confidence, it will also give you the best clues as to the atmosphere of the interview. What is the facial expression of the interviewer? Smiling or severe, bored or excited? Knowing this will help you, whereas keeping your gaze lowered will project an impression of timidity and lose you the chance to gain valuable information. When you go to the rest room before or during the interview process, it is worth ensuring that your hands are dry and warm – use the hand-dryers available. Some interviewers consider a cold, clammy handshake to be a sign of a nervous or suspicious character!

Background reading

It is as well, no matter what job you are applying for, to have read at least today's newspaper (paper or website) and preferably an analytical weekly like *The Economist*, *New Scientist*, *Time* or *Newsweek* or similar so that you are reasonably well briefed on what is going on. The interviewer will probably not start directly on your résumé (although a few do). More likely the interviewer will start with a minute or two of general discussion – and whatever is news today or this week is likely to be a good topic.

The interviewer may think that they are not making judgements during this time, but they probably are – and you can help yourself by being well briefed on current subjects of the day – including sport if this is important to you (and sometimes even if it is not!). And relax – that is what the interviewer wants you to do anyway. Don't be like some candidates and wonder why the interviewer is asking them about yesterday's sporting event – they are not testing your general knowledge, just trying to make you feel at ease.

It's all immensely good experience anyway. Any exercises or interviews you have already done will stand you in good stead – you may get something along the same lines again. It should be good fun provided the interviews are well conducted. After all, the interviewers also have to sell their organisation to you – for all they know you will be choosing between them and a competitor.

It's even better if you have two or more interviews with different organisations already arranged (which is why it's a good idea to get lots of applications off at about the same time). You can then have a positive perspective on each of them, and do not regard each interview as your only chance. But even if you only have one interview to attend at this stage, try a mind game: imagine that you have at least one more interview with another company to attend soon after, or even one that is likely to result in a job offer. This may well be all you need to give you a feeling of being in control – of you being the one choosing which organisation to work for. With this sense of confidence, you will probably perform better at interview.

Coping with a bad interviewer

If you **do** have a truly awful interviewer, who just throws questions at you seemingly at random, does not listen to your answers, and takes delight in talking about his or her own favourite subjects, don't be disappointed if you do not receive a job offer. You may or you may not – in that situation the odds are random. There is not much you can do about it, but don't on any account let it get you down – you've simply drawn a poor interviewer. During the interview you should keep trying to bring the discussion round to what you have done, listen carefully and by all means ask what the job requires. If the interviewer gives you a satisfactory answer, then bring out those aspects of your résumé that fit this, but if they are really a bad interviewer, they will probably not listen anyway. Put it down to experience; certainly write a short letter expressing your disappointment, not just at not getting the job, but more particularly at the poor quality of the interview – but after this get on with other applications. Most organisations thankfully are more professional.

10.7 PANEL INTERVIEWS

In some cases, an organisation may use a panel interview. This involves a number of people from the organisation (sometimes including a member of the recruitment agency or a head-hunter) interviewing one candidate – you. This can appear threatening – you walk into a room and are faced by two, three sometimes up to eight people. Don't be put off by this – the trick is to know why the organisation is using a panel interview. Because at first sight it is not a very clever way for an organisation to arrange an interview. For example, suppose there is a four-person panel interview, which lasts one hour. If, instead of having a panel interview, each panel member interviewed you individually, the organisation would collect four hours of evidence from you, instead of just one hour. So why do some organisations use panel interviews?

There are a number of related reasons. Sometimes you are only available for one hour (perhaps during your lunch break), so this is the only way that the four people who will have to decide on whether to employ you can all see you. But the most usual reason is to ensure that all divisions who will be affected by the job have input into the decision to hire, so they support the hiring decision, and can't say that they didn't agree with it. It also helps to minimise favouritism, eg one interviewer may select a candidate whom he or she likes, for whatever reason, rather than the most competent. It also helps that all the panel see the identical evidence – you – for the duration of the interview, and have a chance to ask the questions they want. Put this way, you can regard a panel interview as an opportunity to get a good start in your job, and a chance to impress all the decision-makers at the same time.

The structure of panel interviews

Panel interviews are sometimes well structured, so for example there may be a 'Chair' who will introduce members of the panel to you, and each panel member may concentrate on a particular area of competence. But there are also panel interviews which are much less structured. In this case, you may well need to take the lead to ensure that all the positive evidence you want to present is talked about – you should feel able to draw the panel's attention to this if they seem to be missing it.

In many ways you have the advantage over the panel – you control and co-ordinate the way you present yourself and the way you answer. Whereas, after you have attended a few panel interviews, you will notice that often the panel's questions become quite unco-ordinated, and the members sometimes struggle to present questions clearly and in an ordered way. You may also notice that not all members of the panel listen as carefully to your answers.

So don't be overawed by panel interviews – they may not be the most efficient method of selection, but they certainly should allow you to present most of your positive evidence.

10.8 TELEPHONE INTERVIEWS

In the USA, some organisations may be up to 4,000 miles away from where you are working or studying. Although they could fly you for interview, and often do, this is (a) costly (either to you or the organisation – both unfortunate); (b) time consuming; and (c) may mean that the first possible date for interview is a month away or more. Wouldn't it make more sense to interview candidates over the phone?

And that is exactly what some organisations do, in the USA and to a lesser extent in Europe. Usually there is a preliminary call to arrange a suitable time, then the interviewer will telephone you, establish that the time is convenient for you to speak freely, and the interview will proceed as if you are in the same room. It would be unusual for a telephone interview to be the final stage of selection, but it can certainly be used to determine who proceeds to the final stage.

Are telephone interviews as accurate as face-to-face interviews? I tested this, using candidates who agreed to be interviewed twice, once on the telephone, again face to face (some had the telephone interview first, some had it second). The conclusion was that properly conducted telephone interviews gave very similar results to face-to-face interviews.

How should you prepare for a telephone interview? Pretty much the same as for a face-to-face interview, except that you need to pay very careful attention to:

- being in a place where you can speak freely – it is no good trying to speak from a communal phone where everyone else is chatting around you, and you find it difficult to hear the interviewer; even worse if you try to do it from work, when your organisation does not know you are applying for other jobs. You really have to be able to speak freely – if not it is better not to have the interview on the phone.

- choosing where you get the best connection, especially if you are using a mobile or wireless phone, and especially if using Skype voice over internet.

- ensuring you have a copy of your résumé in front of you, as the interviewer may well refer to some aspects of it; also have your notes and examples of competencies you have not included in your résumé, and blank sheet of paper for your notes – for example if you are asked to cover four areas, you may want to note down the four areas you come up with, so that you cover them in a clear, consistent way. You really should consider drawing up an Interview Preparation Table (10.3 and Appendix 6) if you haven't already done one. This will indicate the most likely interview questions (look especially here for the competencies the organisation says they will be looking for) and prompt you with a four-column table or matrix, with the left-hand column containing the sample question, and the next three columns your example answers: A (best), B (second best – in case you have already used your A), and C (in case you have already used both A and B). Use enough bullet points to remind you of all the evidence you want to give. Since it is a telephone interview, the interviewer can't see this (and anyway, even if they could your preparation is positive not negative). When they ask a competency question you can say (while you look for the right example), 'Just a minute ...' You will be surprised how natural and complete your answers will be.

- being comfortable – the interview may last for up to one hour, so if you are comfortable with a speaker phone, this may be a good way to do it; or practise with a speaker phone or hands-free phone. If not, at least have comfortable seating.

- trying to visualise the interviewer, and speaking to them just as you would to a friend on the phone – be positive, confident, smile, move around a bit within the limits of the phone. After all, the job of the interviewer is to help you to present your best evidence.

If all the logistics are just not possible, say so when they try to arrange the telephone interview. It may be possible for you to go to a local office of the organisation and use the phone from there. Indeed, this may even allow use of a web-cam or similar if there is a conference room set up for this.

11
Psychometric tests

Psychometric tests used for selection fall into four main groups:

- personality measures;
- ability or cognitive measures;
- interest measures (these are mainly used for career choice);
- team- or group-based measures.

Almost all start with a few sample questions, with answers that are not marked, to help you to get a clear idea of the type of question, and the answers they are looking for. There are literally hundreds of psychometric tests available to both organisations and individuals. Some are traditional paper copies, to be filled in by hand, usually on a pre-printed form which aids scoring – but increasingly they are available on PCs, often online. Most are well researched and developed, but some have at best only face validity, ie they may look as though they produce results that are reliable and predictive, but there is no proof that they actually do so. Surprisingly, some organisations use psychometric tests that fall into this category – you may choose not to complete their tests, but then you will probably not be considered for employment.

Many assessment centres include psychometric measures, both ability (cognitive) and personality, so it is a good idea to get used to them as early as possible; and many organisations use them for a variety of team building or other activities.

In the UK and other countries, many organisations use a large international psychology consultancy called SHL to provide them with their psychometric tests. You can get some practice and feedback on psychometric tests at *www.shldirect.com* for example.

11.1 PERSONALITY MEASURES

Personality measures questions do not really have a right or wrong answer, so relax and enjoy them, and look forward to receiving the feedback you should get. The best ones can be very interesting and insightful. Examples of these are the Myers-Briggs, and Firo-B, but there are literally hundreds. In some personality measures the feedback you are given may be a bit spurious – if you look carefully at the questions and how you have answered them, you may well find that the feedback is little more than a synopsis or summary or rewording of the way in which you answered the questions. But the best personality measures are based on careful factor analysis and are carefully validated.

The use of personality measures in selection depends critically on a clear and accurate identification of the type(s) of personality who perform well in that particular job or career. Given the wide variety of personalities who are successful in most careers or jobs, and the myriad interactions between people in teams, this is seldom available. In particular, some studies of successful teams have identified the need for a diversity of roles and personalities in teams – packing teams full of what is perceived to be **the** best personality type frequently leads to bitter conflict as each competes for the preferred role, until some start to perform out of character in their second preferred role.

Nonetheless personality measures are popular, and are usually introduced 'as additional evidence that assessors can take into account'. Used in this way, and provided the candidates are given proper feedback, personality measures can be useful in selection.

To take a very simple example, if you tend towards being an introvert, then perhaps a role that requires you to meet lots of new people and to gain new clients by extensive networking may not be the best for you or for the organisation that may employ you. It is likely that you recognise this yourself without the need for psychometrics. However, if you feel that the personality measure has wrongly identified you, then you should be able to produce evidence and examples that demonstrate this.

Does personality change?

It is difficult to say how long a personality measure remains accurate. After all, does your personality stay the same? We all know people whose personality has changed – sometimes after a stressful time or significant event(s), but also after a number of years in a job that requires a particular type of personality. Introverts can sometimes take on an extrovert role at work because they have to in order to succeed. Sometimes the new 'personality' will stay with them, sometimes they will revert to introvert when they are away from work. The feedback they get from their partner or family members will be a key factor in whether or not their personality changes.

Either way, as a very rough guide, personality measures probably have a shelf life of five years – after that it makes sense not to place too much faith in the results – your personality will probably have changed over that time.

There have been a number of analyses combining various studies which try to show the accuracy with which psychometrics and other selection methods predict subsequent job performance. Generally personality measures do not usually predict subsequent job performance very well – for the reasons given (see Appendix 3). However, psychometric measures of ability do much better, as do properly structured interviews, and assessment and development centres.

11.2 ABILITY OR COGNITIVE TESTS

You may well recognise these as general IQ or intelligence tests. There are also some ability tests that measure more specific abilities – for example skill or aptitude in programming. In fact these tests may well give some people their best possible chance of getting the job that is suited to them. So welcome them. The ability tests you are likely to come across are approximately 40% numerical, 40% shapes (eg you must identify the next shape in the sequence) and 20% verbal (eg verbal reasoning – is the statement logical or not?).

People who are shy may welcome the chance to show just how good they are in a setting that enables them to interact with a computer, or anyway just paper – particularly if the work they are applying for also requires this.

Because of the emphasis on speed, and quick thinking, you should make sure you are feeling particularly wide awake and full of energy for these – certainly get a good night's sleep beforehand. An extra cup of coffee or two may give you a better chance of doing well than partying the night before and waking with a hangover. However, some people find that the caffeine in coffee decreases performance (perhaps because caffeine can make you so hyperactive that you miss things and/or are more easily persuaded). Others find energy (glucose) drinks increase performance – for example Lucozade Sport. This is particularly important for assessment centres which last a whole day – you may want to bring two or three energy drinks and sip throughout the day. You will have to find out what works best for you.

If the test is online, some applicants may consider having a friend work with them to help – sort of 'phone a friend' except that the friend can be in the same room as you. Organisations would prefer that you do not do this, and may even require it. In practice though it is likely that you will lose more time discussing which answer to put than you will gain in accuracy. Of more value will be your friend's experience and feedback to you if they have already taken the test – the questions will almost certainly be randomised and changed from candidate to candidate, but you can benefit from getting a general idea of what is likely to be asked.

Example cognitive or ability questions

There are a number of websites which provide example questions (see Appendix 12) and most university careers services provide a service which includes example tests you can try yourself. This is well worth doing, as most people will improve their scores with some practice – but there is a limit to this improvement. Just to give you an idea of what to expect, and whether it is worth practising, here are a few examples to show you the type of questions you may be asked. Tests are timed, and include at least 20 and often many more questions. All tests vary, so the ones you may be given will be different from these questions, but they will give you a rough idea. Answers are given at the end of this chapter, with a brief indication of the reasoning.

Example numerical analysis

Consider the following table which is based on the United Nations Millennium Targets. It shows for some regions of the world the percentage of population who had an income of less than US$1/day, and percentage of women aged 15–24 who were literate. Then answer the questions below:

Region	Population (millions)	% below $1/day 1990	% below $1/day 2004	% women 15–24 who were literate 1990	% women 15–24 who were literate 2004
N Africa and W Asia	386	2.2	2.7	55*	72*
Middle Africa	104	44.6	46.4	60	69
Latin America and Caribbean	546	11.3	9.5	93	96
East Asia	1507	33.0	16.6	93	99
Southern Asia	1560	39.4	29.9	51	63
SE Asia and Oceania	573	19.6	10.2	93**	95**

* excludes W Asia; ** excludes Oceania

1 Which region had the second highest percentage of people living below $1/day in 1990?

A N Africa and W Asia;
B Middle Africa;
C Latin America and Caribbean;
D Eastern Asia;
E Southern Asia;
F SE Asia and Oceania.

2 Which region has achieved the greatest reduction in total number of people living on less than $1/day between 1990 and 2004?

A N Africa and W Asia;
B Middle Africa;

C Latin America and Caribbean;
D Eastern Asia;
E Southern Asia;
F SE Asia and Oceania.

3 What is the number of people living below \$1/day in the combined regions of Northern Africa and West Asia, and Middle Africa in 2004?

A 58.7 million;
B 69.4 million;
C 31.5 million;
D 98.5 million;
E 5.87 million;
F 75.8 million.

4 Which region has achieved the greatest percentage increase in literacy in women aged 15–24 from 1990–2004?

A N Africa;
B Middle Africa;
C Latin America and Caribbean;
D Eastern Asia;
E Southern Asia;
F SE Asia.

Example numerical sequences

What is the next number in this sequence?

0, 3, 8, 15, 24, ?

Example shapes

a and b are sets of three shapes. Which of c, d or e follows the same sequence?

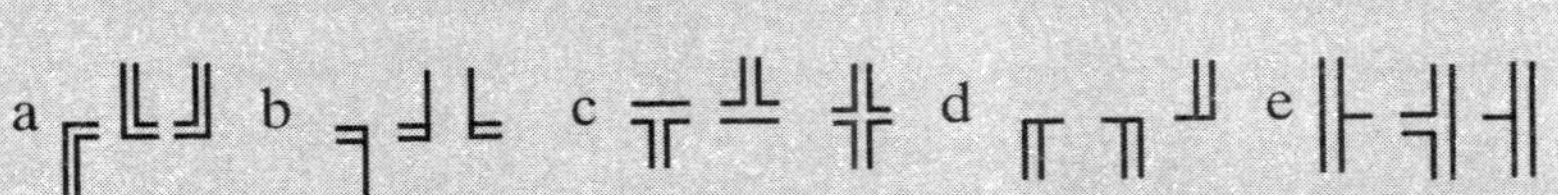

(Another type of shape test involves folding boxes to see which pattern would be on a particular face.)

Example verbal reasoning

Consider the following paragraph:

> Skyscrapers need a rare combination of factors to come together if they are to make money. The main ones are a short supply of land in a desirable location (like Hong Kong), building restrictions that preserve this scarcity, and easy access to finance. Other factors like bedrock near the surface to drive foundations into (like New York) help to keep costs down. But nature can be mastered: Chicago, home to the first skyscrapers, sits on mud, Dubai's giant towers are being built on sand.

Using only the information in the paragraph, please evaluate whether the following sentences are:

1 Definitely true;

2 Definitely untrue;

3 Probably true (ie more likely to be true than not);

4 Probably untrue (ie more likely to be untrue than true);

5 Insufficient data – there is not enough information in the statement to tell.

a There are only a few situations in which building a skyscraper can be justified.
b The first skyscrapers were built in New York.
c If there are two skyscrapers, one built on rock and the other built on mud, then the one built on mud cost less to build.
d Skyscrapers built in desirable locations will make money.
e Dubai's giant skyscrapers will make money.

11.3 INTEREST MEASURES

Interest measures are usually used to help with career choice, so you are the client. They may check out the activities you are interested in, and compare them with the interests identified by people in thousands of different occupations. The presumption is that if your interests are similar to those of people in certain occupations, then it is likely that you may also enjoy those occupations. They certainly will give you a starting list of occupations to consider. These types of measures are usually available from psychologists, or career advisers. One of the most common is the Campbell Interest and Skills Inventory – this includes a self-reported skills section, but is limited in the number of jobs it covers, and can be seen as too American based.

11.4 TEAM OR GROUP MEASURES

Probably the best known of these was developed by Belbin. Essentially he identified that teams or groups need members who play different roles if they are to function successfully. So a team composed of members who are all of the same personality type, or who all try to play the same role, will not be as successful as one in which all the required roles are represented. For example, a team with eight people, each of whom tries to be leader, will not be as effective as one in which some people concentrate on generating ideas, or getting resources, or helping others, or looking after the decision-making process. Insights from these measures are helpful during interviews when you are asked what your role specifically is in your present employment, or during group tasks at assessment centre (see 13.8). In particular, don't think that selectors are only looking for leadership behaviour.

11.5 ANSWERS TO EXAMPLE ABILITY QUESTIONS

Numerical analysis

1 E Southern Asia (39.4% – taken directly from the table).

2 D East Asia. Multiplying the percentage reduction from 1990 to 2004 (16.4%) by the population (1507) gives a reduction of 247 million, which is more than any other region. You could do the sum for all the regions, but this would take time, and you can probably estimate that East Asia has the greatest reduction in percentage of poverty, and almost the largest population, so it must have the largest absolute reduction.

3 A For Northern Africa and Western Asia region, the number is 2.7% of 386 million (10.42 million); and for Middle Africa, 46.4% of 104 million (48.25 million) so the answer is 58.67 million.

4 A North Africa, an increase from 55% to 72%. Note the region definition is changed for this statistic.

Numerical sequence

35. The progression is x squared + ascending even numbers, starting from x = 0. So the sequence is 0 squared + 0; 1 squared + 2; 2 squared + 4; 3 squared + 6; 4 squared + 8; and 5 squared + 10 (35).

Shapes d

The trio of shapes in both a and b have the first shape rotated to produce the third shape, and 'flipped' (turned over) to produce the middle shape. Only d follows this pattern. (You could be even simpler and note that a, b, and d all have shapes which can be transformed (rotated or flipped) to form each other, whereas c and e have different shapes.)

Verbal reasoning

a Definitely true. The statement says that it takes a rare combination of factors – so in only a few situations will building a skyscraper be justified.

b Definitely untrue. The statement says that the first skyscraper was built in Chicago.

c Probably untrue. The statement says that building a skyscraper on rock close to the surface helps to keep costs down, but there are many other costs involved, for example size, location and when the skyscraper was built, so the one on mud may actually have cost less to build.

d Probably true. A desirable location is a positive factor but if there are few or no planning restrictions for example then other land will also be desirable and may mean that the skyscraper does not make money.

e Insufficient data. The statement says nothing about whether the Dubai towers will make money (just that the cost of building is greater than if they were built on rock).

12
Dinner and other informal events

Dinner the night before should give you a good chance to see how well you get on with your future colleagues. They will probably offer you lots of wine and spirits. You know how many glasses of wine get you alert and going, and how many reduce you to a bad state. If you are offered a drink before dinner it may be better just to have a soft drink, then a glass of water at the table, and if you drink alcohol (and if you don't, just say no), have a glass of wine at dinner, maybe two. Or just have two or three beers instead of wine – they are easier to count – no liquors, or port. That way you will avoid a splitting headache the next day which is when the important exercises take place.

12.1 IS DINNER PART OF THE ASSESSMENT?

It's worth checking on the organisation's website whether the dinner is part of the assessment or not. Many large organisations genuinely don't get any feedback from the people who attend the dinner, although some undoubtedly do. However, the main purpose of the dinner is to help you to relax and get a good impression of the organisation in a non-threatening envionment. So use the opportunity to become familiar with the people without feeling that you have to be 'on show'.

If you are staying overnight, checking out of hotels can take more time than you think (often when you are running late), so allow ten minutes for this. Usually the organisation will pay the bill, but you may be expected to pay for phone calls etc and it can take time for the hotel to check that you haven't made any!

12.2 IF IT IS NOT PART OF THE ASSESSMENT

If the dinner is not assessed, relax; use it to learn more about the organisation, and what makes their approach different. The dinner may be in the organisation's office itself (most companies have dining rooms for management events), so the food should be good, perhaps a bit 'formal'.

It's a good idea to find out if your dinner hosts are the assessors for tomorrow or not. Ask what sort of people they find are successful, and ask too how the people with you at dinner got into the organisation – if they went through an assessment centre, by all means ask if they have any advice on it. The assessment exercises will have changed a bit from when they did it, but probably not a lot. Look through the exercises you will do tomorrow and you will find there is quite a bit of input they can give you. For example, do the selectors look for extreme win/lose positions, or do they prefer well thought out positions that consistently make money? Do they look for an international viewpoint or a local, domestic one? Do they look for a person who negotiates hard and long to get the best price, or do they think that it's often better just to get on with it and take the price offered after, say, one minute of negotiation?

Sometimes organisations offer a site visit, or other informal event, before or after assessments or interviews. In most cases they are trying to 'sell' their organisation to you, so you have everything to gain by attending, and learning as much as you can about the organisation, its business and how it goes about it. You are almost certainly not being assessed so it's safe and more profitable anyway to relax, enjoy it, and learn a lot.

13
Final stage selection and assessment centres

Assessment centres are designed to be the most accurate method of selection so far devised, by analysing the work that is involved in the job or career you are applying for, and then developing exercises that are sufficiently similar to the work. The idea is then that if you do well in the exercises, you will also do well in the job or career. Put this way, assessment centres are likely to be more accurate than most interviews. To take a very simple example, if you want to know whether someone is a good salesman, are you likely to get better evidence by sitting them down and interviewing them – or by giving them a product and product information, giving them 30 minutes to prepare, then asking them to sell to a 'customer' (perhaps an employee of the organisation who has been trained to respond in typical customer ways)?

How assessment centres started

Assessment centres started with the military. They found that candidates who at interview could give good answers on how they would lead people into combat, often failed dismally when they were actually required to do this. Clearly the military needed a situation which gave the candidates a better test of what is actually required. They could then hire those with the required skills, and reject others who might interview well but did not have the skills involved in leadership.

If an organisation asks you to attend an assessment centre, it is probable that they will give some information on their website or other literature on what they are looking for in candidates, and the structure of the assessment centre. Or they may provide this in an attachment to the letter or email inviting you. This is your first step in preparing – knowing what they want, and working out what is the best evidence you can give them on this, and how you can provide this in the exercises.

13.1 EXERCISES TO EXPECT

If the organisation doesn't give information on their assessment centre, it's fair to ask, but they may still refuse to tell you much, if anything. Fortunately there has been a survey of the exercises in assessment centres held by small, medium and large organisations in the UK. Bear in mind that these things change, but it will give you an idea.

Size of organisation:

Exercise	Small %	Medium %	Large %	Total %
Interview	97	97	97	97
Ability measure	89	91	91	91
Personality measure	80	83	79	80
Group discussion	67	79	89	79
Case study	49	64	71	62
Presentation	54	59	61	58
In-tray	19	38	48	35

T Keenan, 'Graduate Recruitment in Britain: a survey of selection methods used by organisations', *Journal of Organisational Behaviour*, 1995, Volume 16, Pages 303–17.

Any team exercises, debates and presentations you have undertaken at school, university, in a sports team, at church, or at work amount to some of the best preparation you can get. But generally organisations are likely to appreciate people who present their evidence confidently and clearly, taking the time needed, but without making a big deal about it (ie not exaggerating), and who listen carefully to others.

13.2 ENJOYING THE EXPERIENCE

The exercises may come in any order (you should be given a timetable on the day, if not before). Arrive at the location 15 minutes early so you can relax when you are there; you will do better if you are more relaxed. Most candidates think they are in competition with others. In fact, usually the organisation has enough places that if all the candidates are good they will make offers to all; if none are good they will make no offers. So it's actually best to think of it as a team exercise and try to help others a bit. However, you still have to take the lead in generating ideas and ways to do things etc yourself!

Advance knowledge

It generally pays to find out as much as you can about the exercises at all points of the process. So this starts with friends or acquaintances who already work with the organisation – they will not only tell you about the 'culture' and feel of the organisation and the type of work, they may also tell you something of the assessment centre exercises. Then there are the hosts at the dinner which is often arranged the night before (see Chapter 12). The organisation should give you a brief one-sentence description of the exercises in the communication inviting you to the assessment centre, and there may also be something on their website.

Finally, you can ask candidates at the same assessment centre, especially if they have just finished an exercise that you are about to start. Be careful here though, some organisations specifically forbid such talk. However, others may feel it is a bit hard to forbid all talk, so a gentle 'How was it?' or 'What did they ask you?' is probably in order. Some candidates may feel that you are a competitor and say nothing, or even try to feed you misleading information, but usually you will get a valuable insight into what to expect, and even some of the questions you are likely to be asked after the exercise by the assessors.

All assessment centres are different, and change over time, but they usually include the following exercises, although some may have only three or four, and others may have different variations.

13.3 BUSINESS SIMULATIONS

This is a simplified version of a part of the business. You will be given background information, then a number of opportunities and events, often in a series of phases or rounds. This may well be run on a PC. The main requirement will be to be organised, try to develop a strategy that you can defend, be alert to opportunities and how to make the most of them, and especially risks and how to minimise them. (Think of spreading the risk over time, over places, or over different organisations, or buying insurance or hedging for example.) New information will probably come in (they will probably feed you some news items as you go along, eg the Fed or the Bank of England has just lowered the base rate by 0.5%, there have been more explosions in Iraq near the oil pipelines, etc).

After the exercise, they will probably ask **why** you made some decisions, so try to have a reason for your actions, rather than 'It just seemed like a good idea.' In some ways this will probably be more important than the actual decisions. You may lose money in the simulation (if this is part of it) but still do well if they are impressed by your answers and why and how you took the decisions, so don't be swayed by losses, and try hard to explain clearly your thinking.

13.4 PRESENTATIONS

You may be asked to bring a presentation with you, or you may be given a subject at the assessment centre. If you are asked to bring one, it could well be based on your degree or experience so far. Perhaps you have already given a presentation that you are confident with; or you may prepare one specially focused on the organisation you are applying to. If you have already given many presentations, you will not need any further advice. If you have not, then choose a subject you are interested in, briefly describe it, then follow the structure suggested later in this section.

If you are given the subject on the day, it will probably be non-specialist technical/financial – after all, some attendees may not be sufficiently familiar with the business of the organisation to enable them to give a detailed technical or financial presentation. See Appendix 10 for an example. And anyway, given the varied backgrounds of the candidates, most organisations will try to 'level the playing field' by setting a subject that everyone will be equally familiar with. It may be from a work setting, but non-specialist, perhaps something like what the company's policy should be on the private use of emails and the web, or whether open-plan offices are more efficient, or whether to give incentives to all sales staff or traders equally, based on team results, or to each employee individually, or something along those lines.

Usually you are given up to 20 minutes for a presentation prepared beforehand, or five to ten minutes for one you have had to prepare at the assessment centre. There are usually only one or two assessors (although occasionally there are more), so it is more of a discussion than a big lecture/presentation. They will probably listen to your presentation, then ask questions afterwards. There is usually no right or wrong answer, just have a good structure to what you want to say, and be prepared to answer questions as clearly and confidently as you can.

They may give you Microsoft PowerPoint, but probably not. If not, you can sometimes use an A4 sheet or flip chart (one or two) to illustrate your points (and give you a structure for your thoughts). If you have PowerPoint don't use more than, say, four to eight slides, or a maximum of one slide every two minutes. As an example:

1 Define the subject or problem.
2 What should be the goal or objective.
3 Analysis of causes, opportunities and risks.
4 The various options.
5 Which option you have chosen and why.
6 (briefly) How to implement, resources required, and any possible sensitivities or risks (eg unintended consequences).

13.5 INTERVIEWS

Most assessment centres include at least one interview to pick up on points not covered by the other exercises. Whereas earlier interviewers will probably have been HR professionals or younger staff, at assessment centres, the interviewers are more likely to be senior managers who may be your department manager or partner if they accept you. So there is a large element for both you and the interviewer of: 'Would I want to spend six hours in an airport lounge or client's waiting room with this person?', as well as an assessment of your abilities.

Smile

So if you want the job (and after all that is why you are there), lighten up a bit, smile, and try to channel your excess energy into being animated and enthusiastic, and fun to be with rather than nervous or even just competent. They may be senior, but they need you just as much as you need them, and if all goes well, they could end up as your mentor. You don't really have anything to lose -- all they can do is not offer you a job, and no other potential employers will know that (unless you choose to tell them).

Final stage interviews are more likely to be conducted by more than one interviewer – don't worry about this, it is often a function of the design of the assessment centre. Just check back on the advice in Chapter 10 on handling panel interviews (10.7). In particular, focus only on the person who has asked you the most recent question. Apart from this, the interviews are likely to be similar to previous interviews, so expect 'Give me an example' type questions, and expect them to probe – perhaps even more deeply. Stick to the facts, just as before, and make sure you have a copy of your résumé and/or online application to remind yourself of what evidence they already have. If you prepared an Interview Preparation Table of competency answers (see 10.3) bring this as well.

Estimate type questions

Questions asking you to make an estimate of something are common at this stage – for example, 'Please tell me how you would estimate how many mobile phones there are in this country.' Approach this by structuring the problem, and being prepared to give alternatives. For example you could say: 'I would approach the major mobile phone networks and ask them how many customers each has, or I could possibly find this in their annual report. I would make an estimate of how many people own two mobiles from different networks, and subtract that. Or I could take a sample of people in a representative town, and find out how many have a mobile phone, then take the census number of people in this country and scale the result up from my sample.' It is less important that you are instantly right, than that you show you can think on your feet, you are not afraid of estimating, and you are oriented to action (ie you don't just say 'I would ask my research department').

Wider implications and risk type questions

Some organisations have specific types of questions to assess whether candidates can recognise the more strategic and less obvious implications of various events. This is based on an appreciation that successful senior executives need to do this, so they want to check potential recruits' ability to do the same. You may be asked to identify the wider implications or opportunities and risks inherent in a particular event.

To answer these types of questions, try to think of a good *Economist* or newspaper article. In addition to the facts and analysis, a good article will also consider the wider implications (think of them as website or blog links). For example, most major events have implications for the environment, the economy, taxation, insurance, employment, education, transport and politics. Use this as a starting check-list, or just work through various scenarios that could reasonably happen, and you will do fine.

You may find that you can get some subtle feedback from the assessors as to whether you are on the right track. After giving a partial answer, look up and check their expressions. If they are absorbed, making notes, you are probably doing OK. If not, it may be worth asking if there is any particular angle they have in mind, to give you better direction.

Questions concerning future development

Remember there is probably a graduate programme, and the interviewers may also be assessing you for other positions than the one you applied for, eg your potential for more senior positions later. So don't be too dogmatic about only wanting to do whatever you applied for – demonstrate that you have breadth of vision and ambition, show an interest in other parts of the organisation, be enthusiastic.

They may ask you about other companies you have applied to. Say something along the lines of 'Well, you were my first application and this is my first assessment centre. I have been to some interviews but nothing definite yet – and anyway you are my first choice.' No need to volunteer information about rejections you may have received. In one sense it is none of their business, and they cannot check it anyway.

13.6 ABILITY AND/OR PERSONALITY MEASURES

If you have already taken these, you may not have to do more – or the organisation may ask you to do a different, perhaps longer set of measures. Either way, examine Chapter 11 on psychometrics for advice on how to approach these.

13.7 IN-TRAY/CASE STUDY EXERCISES

See Appendix 8 for an example in-tray exercise, and Appendix 9 for an example response. You may be given both an in-tray or e-tray and a case study, although you may have just one. An in-tray or e-tray exercise consists of lots of seemingly random documents presented as if they were correspondence that had arrived in someone's in-tray – hence the name. The documents are usually paper although they might be on a PC, in which case the exercise is sometimes called an e-tray. Often there will be some additional information fed in at a later stage.

You are usually given a role, eg your boss has gone on holiday and asked you to look through their mail, and deal with it as necessary until they come back. You will be asked to present your results to the assessors and they will ask you questions on them. They are testing how well you do if you are not spoonfed information, and there is some real risk around – in this case the assessors.

The best approach to in/e-trays

Usually the best approach is to look quickly through the pack of information in four to five minutes – **no more**, to get a feel for what there is, and to see if anything looks very urgent, and if any bits connect with others. Then go through more slowly, sorting the documents into categories – both by subject, and by whether or not they need action. If your papers were stapled together you may need to unstaple them (but keep organised – eg make sure they are placed in different piles, or plastic envelopes, or colour coded etc. A structure that often works is the following:

1 Some items will be important and require action; spend 60% of your time on these.

2 Some items will be urgent but not important – for example office or communication matters; spend 20% of your time on these.

3 Some items will be important, but not require urgent action; spend 20% of your time on these.

4 Some items do not appear to be important or require action. Do not consider these further, except to be aware of the information they contain which may impact on other items.

Prioritise

You need to focus on the important and urgent, and take clear decisions on what to do. Then take what should be quick action on the urgent but not important items (often all that is required is to ask the secretary or someone else to do something, eg change the date of an appointment). Then see if there is any issue in the important non-urgent items for which action can be started now, eg set up a study on it, or ask someone to prepare a recommendation on it within one week.

For the important and urgent items, you probably need to think about the resources available to you (money, people), the main risks, be prepared to arrange a meeting of the people who need to know, be prepared to be decisive on matters that need action now. Consider all the sensitivities and long-term consequences you can, and how to minimise them, and the risks. Remember you are acting for your boss, so you are expected to take decisions. As you go through the items, make up your own mind on what needs to be done. You might even summarise this on an A4 sheet of paper, or write on top of each document. Be confident but not dictatorial!

The best approach to case studies

As an alternative to the in-tray, the case study may be presented as a single briefing document, or two or even three. In this case, the information is all there, but it may well be buried in a lot of largely irrelevant facts, just like the in-tray format. Your approach is essentially the same. You have to decide what is important, prioritise, recognise sensitivities and risks that will probably not be spelled out, but which are implied in the way the subject is presented. You must then come to a conclusion or plan of action, and be prepared to present this clearly.

Use your common sense

For investment banks and other financial organisations, the case study may well involve a description of an organisation, and require analysis – often of its value, and what it should do to increase this. The test here is usually whether you can analyse the strategic opportunities and risks in both detail and in the wider picture. If you have done an MBA or some business or economics courses, you will be expected to make at least a start at this. Even if you have a background in engineering or science you may be asked to do this. Your assessors know that your knowledge of the techniques will be limited, so they are really testing your common sense – so use it, have confidence, think widely, always ask yourself: 'What are the **real** risks involved here, what are the **real** opportunities?'

If you have done an MBA or similar you need to be able to use DCF (discounted cash flow), analyse market multiples (valuing firms by commonly accepted valuation techniques like 2 × earnings or sales or assets for example), financial ratios like the liquidity test, ROACE, P/E ratios etc, risk analysis including probability of loss, total loss, maximum acceptable loss etc. If you are applying for technical positions you may expect to be asked to use numerical or analytical techniques.

These will require quantitative approaches – but that is what you must expect if you are applying to these organisations. It is well worth while practising a few of the above approaches before you attend the assessment. Remember to use a variety of approaches – there is no one correct method.

13.8 GROUP EXERCISES

This is the exercise that many candidates feel most nervous about – probably because the other exercises are in some ways similar to an exam, but a group exercise is not so familiar. However, if you think about it, most business is conducted in meetings or with other people, and many activities at university involve other people. An example group exercise is given in Appendix 11.

Group discussions fall into one of three categories: specific roles, where everyone has a different role to play depending on the particular brief they are given (for example finance director, CEO etc); everyone is given the same brief, and some of the roles in the group are defined; assumed roles, where everyone is given the same brief, and people decide for themselves what roles to play.

There are many variations: in some, all the candidates are given an exercise to discuss together, observed by assessors; in others, the assessors take part in the discussion themselves, just as if you were in a meeting with them. This second type is more likely if the external candidates already have work experience. In this situation it becomes impractical in many cases to put candidates together, since they do not want others to know they are applying. However, in development centres, since all the internal candidates are likely to know who is under consideration anyway, the whole range of exercises is open.

Four key roles

In most group discussions there are four key roles that most groups end up with: Chair, Writer, Timekeeper and Presenter, although these may be combined. **Chair** guides the process – the flow of the discussion, making sure that everyone has a chance to be heard and that they budget time appropriately and keep to it; **Writer** records what is agreed – often on a large flip chart; **Timekeeper** keeps track of the time, reminding the group of this (the Chair usually then has to get the group to act on this reminder – for example, to agree and move on to the next subject); **Presenter** presents the group's conclusions if this is required. Some group discussions start with a part of the process already set out – often asking the members to read the brief for five minutes, then each in turn to give their ideas. Sometimes they also require the group to decide on roles for themselves.

The four main roles (Chair, Writer, Timekeeper and Presenter) offer you an opportunity to draw attention to the evidence you want the assessors to see. Chair gives you the best opportunity to demonstrate your ability to organise people; Writer reveals your ability to summarise complicated discussions and issues clearly; Timekeeper shows your discipline and attention to detail; and Presenter shows your ability to think quickly and present what will probably be a fairly messy conclusion clearly. If you don't have one of these roles, don't worry – the fifth role is in many ways the most important one: clear-thinking ideas generator.

Treat group discussions just like any team exercise or project. Remember that some of the other people won't be as familiar with the organisation's business as you, so the exercise may well be about something general, eg 'How to improve the image of drug companies or banking', or 'How companies should decide what money to give to charities', or something along those lines.

Behaving naturally

All exercises are a bit artificial, but so are exams and we get used to them. In the group exercise, especially if the assessors are in the same room, observing what is happening, then it can seem even more artificial, and potentially off-putting. However, think of it this way – it is a bit like a courtroom where lots of people are watching as the main lawyers present their case, and try to reach a conclusion. Or a negotiation where many members of a team say little, and just take notes. Or journalists watching politicians or a sports coach. In the group exercise, **you** are one of the main characters, and the assessors are the ones taking notes. If you concentrate hard enough on the problem you have been given, after a while (five minutes) you will find that you forget about the observers and just focus on the other participants.

The main thing is to be sure about what you think should be done, say so clearly and confidently, and listen carefully to what the others have to say. Make notes, and if others have good points incorporate them in what you think should be done. Then help the team come to a decision, present the conclusion if you can, and answer questions. You may find it helpful to distinguish between content and process.

Content and process

Content consists of your ideas about what should be done about the problem presented to you – to start an advertising campaign, or to set an annual budget and categorise the various donations etc. **Process** is how you as a group are going to manage yourselves – usually to arrive at a decision. You have the right to input on both content and process, and one of the key decisions you will have to take for yourself is when to input process, and when to input content. Very often the exercise either explicitly requires each candidate to say something in turn at the start, or this is arrived at by discussion. If this is the case, you can probably contribute both process and content, since this is the first occasion when you will have the chance to speak with everyone listening, and by covering both content and process you will be showing your breadth of thought and influence.

What not to do

Some people think that what they are expected to do in a group exercise is to talk loudly, be decisive with little evidence, override others, and generally exhibit what they think of as 'leadership'. With very few exceptions these people will be marked right down, so don't even think of doing this yourself. Yes, you need to be clear on what you think should be done; yes, you need to stand up for your viewpoint, but it is more important to have listened carefully to what others have to contribute, and to build a better solution, than to try to impose your solution on others.

The problem sometimes is that this type of overbearing person can make what is already an artificial exercise even more artificial as they compete for air-time. If you are in an exercise with such a person, you will need to be forceful with your own viewpoint, insist if necessary on your right to be heard for at least as long as others, and work hard on process issues – for example how the group as a whole is going to decide on what course of action to take (or indeed you can question whether consensus is required).

How group exercises are assessed

The assessors of the group exercise usually concentrate on two or three candidates each – it is difficult to focus on more than this. You will not know who is concentrating on you (although you can take a pretty good guess – it is likely to be the assessor sitting opposite you with a good view of you and what you are doing). But it makes no sense to play to this person – far better just to forget they are there and get on with the content and process issues.

If there is something worth remembering, it is the qualities or criteria that the assessors are looking for. It helps a lot if you know these, because to some extent you can work on exhibiting the desired behaviour in the group exercise. For example, if you know that the organisation is particularly looking for teamwork and analytical skills, then you can concentrate on presenting a clear and well-analysed position, and then on helping and supporting others to arrive at a joint, well-thought-out conclusion.

13.9 ROLE-PLAY

Although they are not included in the survey of assessment centre exercises, a number of organisations use role-play exercises, sometimes employing actors. For example, you may be given a brief to play a manager in the organisation, and the actor or assessor may play the role of a customer who has a problem or complaint. This gives everyone the chance to see at first hand your competence in dealing with situations like this. The actor or assessor will have been asked to play a fairly natural role, not too extreme, so approach this normally, don't think that you have to overdramatise.

Keep the 'customer' satisfied

Try to listen carefully to what the 'customer' is saying, and **show** that you are listening. The most common error is to talk *at* the client, as opposed to making the conversation two-way. For example, in the opening 30 seconds, emphasise: 'I realise you [as the client] know more about this topic than me, I'd like to make this a two-way process … feel free to ask questions at any point … I'll discuss the points as we go.' The most common reason for doing badly in this kind of exercise is making a one-way presentation to the client. This is definitely the case as far as consultancies and banks are concerned, and most other organisations too.

Be aware of the limits of your authority and don't overstep them – the organisation will not be impressed by you offering huge discounts or even giving the product away free, just because a single customer has a problem. You have to work out what the customer is really upset about, and see what ways there are to remedy the situation, without overstepping your authority.

13.10 HOW CANDIDATES ARE ASSESSED AT ASSESSMENT CENTRES

Most candidates at an assessment centre are assessed on the basis of the competencies or criteria that the organisation has identified as important for the jobs under consideration. Usually there will be about four to eight competencies or criteria, and each exercise in the assessment centre will be especially designed to produce good evidence on perhaps half of these, a different set for each exercise. So, for example, a group exercise will probably give good evidence on analytical skill, teamwork, clarity of presentation, and decisiveness (if these are some of the criteria the organisation wants to measure). A presentation may give good evidence on ability to convince others, analytical skill, clarity of presentation, financial expertise etc. The assessors will probably have a rating form for each candidate for each exercise, with the criteria they are expected to assess, and a rating scale, which may be simply A,B,C,D,E, but should have at least some behavioural anchors, ie definitions of some of the behaviours expected from each rating. For example, for analytical skill, the ratings may be as follows.

Rating A: analyses the whole breadth of the problem, taking into account relevant factors that less perceptive observers might miss, then identifies and analyses the important issues in sufficient depth to enable a conclusion, including further information that is needed. Explicitly identifies factors that are irrelevant. Presents numerical analysis where appropriate.

Rating B: analyses the whole problem, but misses some relevant factors, analyses those issues he/she considers to be important in depth, but does not continue the analysis in sufficient depth to arrive at full conclusions. Gets sidetracked by one or two irrelevant issues.

Rating C: analyses about half the problem, but includes a number of irrelevant issues, and fails to go into depth on most of them.

Rating D: tries hard to analyse the problem, but only gets through less than half the issues, and then in insufficient depth. Gets sidetracked by numerous irrelevant issues.

Rating E: analysis is limited to not much more than a re-presentation of the facts already presented in the original problem. Little or no evidence of analysis beyond the obvious.

Most rating forms will encourage the assessors to concentrate on collecting behavioural evidence for each quality or factor during the exercise, and then to rate only after they have collected and considered this evidence. However, untrained, inexperienced or impetuous assessors sometimes make a rating, and then look for evidence to support this. Needless to say, this latter course of action is likely to be less accurate or effective, since the whole point of the assessment centre is to enable candidates to present evidence which will allow a more accurate rating. Making a rating first and then looking for evidence rather defeats the object of this. If you are a candidate, you may be aware that this is happening, but there is not much you can do about it, beyond concentrating on trying throughout the assessment centre to provide as much positive evidence as you can.

The ratings on each competency will probably be weighted and used to arrive at a total, which the assessors will then review; assessments are still not completely objective, and the assessors may adjust the ratings or their decision if they feel this is appropriate. Sometimes there is a minimum rating required for each or some exercises.

You should try to enjoy an assessment; smile, you will probably do well. Some things will be different from what I have described, because I probably didn't design the particular exercises being used. However, the above will give you a rough idea of what to expect and you can cope with the rest easily.

You will find that whatever happens it is really good experience for other assessment centres – many companies use them to decide on promotions as well as recruitment. In that case they are often called development centres.

14
Other selection methods

There are many ways to select people for jobs. First come first served is the simplest – if there is a vacancy that probably most people could fill, then the first person to apply gets the job. This presumes that (a) most people will do the job to the same standard, so why bother with the effort of selection?, and/or (b) it is too difficult to predict who will do well and who will do badly, so you may as well fill the position as quickly as possible.

However, for most jobs the employer probably does have an idea that there are some people who will do better in the job than others, and recognises that if they can just identify who these better people are, then the organisation will be more successful, run more smoothly and make more money.

Cranks and cronies

Enter the weird and wonderful world of the hunch, gut feeling, hypothesis, call it what you will. The employer comes to believe that a certain type of person does well in the job, or that a particular test or set of questions will help them predict who will do well. Examples include analysing candidates' handwriting, asking them to dinner and observing how they behave, giving them practical tests, setting arbitrary age or gender or race criteria (almost all of which have no basis in fact), and so on. The 'old boy network' is a well-developed example of this method. It effectively restricts the choice of candidates to people who are already known. The more modern version is often called 'cronyism'.

Referrals

Referrals are increasingly being used – employees are asked to refer people they know for jobs in the organisation. This has the advantage that much of the initial selection is done – presuming that the referrer only refers people they genuinely think would do well. But it can restrict the circle of people recruited, and – especially if incentives are given for referrals – can be open to abuse. However, it is too attractive a method to ignore.

The better methods lead ultimately to the assessment centre or the practical test of ability. One of the earlier examples already mentioned was the military, who discovered that asking candidates questions in an office did not predict terribly well who would be good at leading troops in battle. So they developed a series of exercises involving a variety of stressful events which required leadership, teamwork and communication, to help them decide who to train to be officers.

Later the same principle was extended to business executives who do not (usually) have to lead their staff into battle, but who often do have to lead them to complete major projects, compete with other companies to win contracts, and communicate with distant subsidiaries thousands of miles away. So the interview is not necessarily the best selection tool available, and exercises, examples, samples of work, vacation work, all are quite properly used in selection. However (if you are the one doing the selection), these methods should all be checked and kept under review; they should at least have the most basic validity, ie they should bear a significant resemblance to the challenges involved in the job or career you are selecting for, and preferably should be based on a clear analysis of what is required to perform the job or career successfully. (As well as being clear on what does **not** affect job performance – for example, age, sex, sexual preference, race etc.)

Vacation jobs

Vacation jobs are increasingly used by organisations as the very best form of assessment centre – after all, the candidate actually works in the organisation for a period, thereby giving lots of evidence on which to base a judgement. The disadvantage is that vacation jobs, unless carefully designed, may not allow a lot of scope for the candidate to show the competencies required, and the candidate's supervisor may also not be completely objective.

Pre-screening

Some organisations who need to recruit very quickly – for example, for projects for which they have bid – pre-screen some candidates so that if the organisation is awarded the contract, they can make offers to people straight away.

Job analysis

If the accuracy of selection is a concern (and it often should be), consultants are available who will, for a fee, analyse the jobs or careers in question, develop with the organisation the criteria probably important for good performance, and develop tests or exercises which will help to predict which candidates are likely to do well. In most jobs the value to the organisation of employing an excellent performer, as opposed to a poor performer, is at least as great as the total cost of employing the consultant for one year. So the payback from a good analysis and development of proper selection methods will be very quick and will continue long after the first employee has done well, been promoted, and another candidate recruited to replace them.

15
Offers and feedback

The best time for employers to make a decision on who to recruit is when they have all the evidence available, and it is fresh in everyone's mind. In other words, straight after the selection process. So, ideally, immediately after examining the résumé, or conducting the interview, or holding the assessment centre, all those involved should get together as necessary and make a decision. And that decision should be communicated to all the candidates as soon as practical, ideally the same or next day. This is not only the ideal, it is probably the approach which is least time-consuming for those involved, as any other method involves looking again at papers, résumés etc, and more communication. So organisations should aim to make a decision on the same day as the selection, and to communicate that decision the next day.

Unfortunately, not all organisations do this, but you as a candidate can reasonably request that this happens, and at least ask when you can expect an answer. The better organisations will also offer feedback. Of course, to the successful candidates, a job offer may well be the only feedback they are interested in. To unsuccessful candidates, however, the feedback may be even more important, and organisations can gain a deserved reputation as professional, by providing even brief feedback.

Companies are sometimes fearful that providing feedback lays them open to negotiation or litigation, along the lines of: 'You say I didn't show enough evidence of clear communication. Well, let me give you some more examples'; or, 'You say that I did not show enough leadership – that is clearly wrong, and I will sue you for it.'

In practice, all candidates are so grateful for prompt, clear feedback that this is the last thing they have in mind, and they may apply again and enter the organisation later, perhaps in a different role.

15.1 TIME LIMITS

Most offers will contain a time limit by which the candidate must respond – because clearly the organisation cannot keep the job open indefinitely while the candidate dithers. Two weeks is usually considered reasonable. Less than this could be construed as unfairly pressuring the candidate, unless there are good reasons.

15.2 WHEN TO DISCUSS SALARY OFFERS AND OTHER ISSUES

When should you discuss money and all the other aspects that go together to make an acceptable remuneration package? Probably the best time for both organisation and individual is during the final interviews. By this time it should be pretty clear to both parties that they are interested in each other, yet neither can take the other for granted. So ask about the expected remuneration package – both employer and individual have everything to gain by getting a better understanding of the other's expectations.

Once an offer has been made in writing, this is usually final – for many organisations this is a policy, because otherwise they may gain a reputation as an organisation that will increase salaries if you just ask. However, there is sometimes room for 'clarification' – examples can include adding a forthcoming general increase; increasing relocation costs, or the value of the car; or even a 'golden hello' (a one-off bonus when you start, which does not affect internal salary relativities but does recognise the risk you are taking in joining). But don't bank on this. If you can, make it clear what you expect, and then the organisation shouldn't make an offer that they know will be rejected – although occasionally organisations will hope that a firm written offer may just tip the balance.

Look also for the sort of coded information that may be given at this stage – for example, from the organisation: 'We would find it difficult to pay a salary in excess of £ — because this would be more than we pay other people you would be working with, but we might be able to do something about the car, and maybe cover all your relocation costs ...' Or from you: 'I would not be able to move for less than I am currently receiving in total, but I am interested in the challenge your organisation is offering, and might be able to start at £ — provided there was a firm commitment to a promotion within 12 months ...' Or even from the organisation: 'In Edinburgh we would not be able to match your salary expectations, but suppose we were to locate you in London, then maybe we could do something ...'

15.3 SALES TALK

Look also for the standard sales talk which goes like this: if you are concerned about money, they will try to talk about quality; if you are concerned about quality, they will talk about money. In other words, if the organisation cannot offer any more than £ — because they have firm pay guidelines which apply to all new graduates without exceptions, expect them to distract you from salary if they can, and talk a lot about the excitement of the job and the potential for huge earnings in the future. And if the organisation has just made some well-publicised business mistakes and has a slightly tarnished reputation, expect them to emphasise the earnings you will get. There is nothing wrong with this, of course. What they are saying may even be true, but recognise it for the tactic that it is, and you are more likely to make judgements that are in your long-term interests.

16
Alternatives to applying direct

There are now almost as many methods of finding employment as there are ways of earning a living. So this book cannot cover all the alternatives – but it does cover most of them.

Going it alone

One alternative that you should seriously consider is self-employment and/or starting your own organisation. This has the advantage that you will definitely get a job (usually the CEO – after all, you are doing the selecting); the disadvantage is that you will probably have to have a well-thought-out business plan. But you may be able to combine ideas with friends and come up with a realistic possibility that will enable you to approach a bank manager or other source of money – or you may be prepared to put some start-up money in yourself. But do check your business plan with at least one other person who can point out any weaknesses in it – it's cheaper to be made aware of these at the planning stage rather than by subsequent events.

Searching the net

If you are still keen to be employed, you might consider sites such as *www.goldjobs.com* or *www.silverjobs.com* which highlight high-paying and high-impact jobs where organisations are keen to attract strong candidates. Sites such as these use the web to offer a very cost-effective alternative to head-hunting.

Specialist agencies

Recruitment agencies play a major role in selection, especially for temporary jobs. Most have online applications and some offer psychometric tests with feedback. Examples include Reed (*www.reed.co.uk*), Hays (*www.hays.com*) and Monster (*www.monster.com*). And there are a large number of agencies which specialise in particular fields. Scientific and technical recruitment agencies often advertise in professional magazines and publications, often those published by national professional associations or chartered institutes. They may well provide you with advice, and will do their best to place you. This is how they earn their money, which ranges from about 10% of your first year's compensation up to as much as 33%. Certainly there is no harm in putting your name with recruitment agencies. You will probably be able to gauge your chances by how keen they are to have you on their books. After all, it is their job to be in close touch with the market, and the supply of and demand for talent.

Inside knowledge

Another option is to join an organisation as a temp, or during your vacation. This gives you an inside knowledge of how the place works and where there may be more permanent and exciting jobs (if that is what you want). Vacation jobs are increasingly used by many top organisations as a means to attract and at the same time assess the best talent (see Chapter 14). Check their websites for dates and opportunities.

Open days

Walk-in or open-day events are worth trying in some circumstances – whether you are applicant or employer. If they are done well, they enable organisations to attract a lot of applicants and screen them in a single day. Sometimes the publicity needed for such events brings in more people than a standard advertisement. And if you are an applicant and you need a job now, you have little to lose.

Conclusion

Finally though, the best way to get that job is to think through your career or job objectives clearly, research the field, spreading the net widely, and prepare a well-thought-out résumé that provides evidence on the competencies most often asked for. Then approach your chosen organisations in as personal and direct a way as you can, and prepare a clear interview preparation table before your interviews.

17
Staying motivated

It is as well to recognise early on that emotions will play a part in your decisions, and some people will gain confidence and get onto a high as the process continues, and others can lose motivation or even get depressed trying to decide what career direction to take, or which companies to apply to. There may seem to be too many choices, controlled by 'other people' or 'suits', and the number of opportunities may itself be daunting. But think of it this way: in this whole world of possibilities there must be some that fit your particular way of thinking, your skills and your approach to work.

When the going gets tough

However, even the most confident and talented person may get depressed by a row of rejections. And the best people *do* receive rejections – partly because they aspire to the more difficult organisations to get into, so they are in competition with other very strong candidates; partly because organisations sometimes (some would say often) have a hiring freeze but don't want to advertise the fact; and partly because the people doing the selection are human and sometimes (again some would say often) make mistakes.

When there is an imbalance of supply and demand, it usually affects all organisations in a similar way, and they react in a similar way – often by freezing recruitment for a period. Since the oversupply of staff may be 10–20%, and organisations typically recruit in the order of 5–10% new staff each year, it can take one to two years before they start recruiting again. Then they often do so in a rush to make up for the lost talent they have missed. These economic depressions may also be a depressing time for you emotionally, but they do have an eventual up side.

It's the same for everyone else, and organisations *will* start recruiting again, although it may mean that you have to spend a year, or even two, in a job that is not your first, second or even third choice. So while it is reasonable to aim for as good a job as those of your friends and colleagues, it is not necessarily a matter for upset or depression when you get the inevitable rejections.

Many people have had 100 rejections and gone on to get excellent jobs. After all, one of the qualities needed to be successful is the ability to keep going when the going gets tough. And people in developed countries have many more opportunities than we sometimes realise. Certainly we have a vastly greater opportunity to find worthwhile, well-paid jobs than people in less fortunate countries.

The crucial factor is whether you are genuinely interested in and motivated by the jobs that you are applying for

If you are, then you must persevere, because your motivation will carry you along and eventually you will get to where you want to be. If you are not really interested in what you are applying for, then it may be worth considering other types of work, especially during periods of economic depression. Consider other angles; roles where perhaps there is more demand, and employers may be hiring more readily. You can always try this, and if you want to switch to something else later, then the work you have already done will stand you in good stead when applying. Or you may find that by chance you have hit on just the work that is right for you. You never know.

17.1 COPING WITH DEPRESSION

Depression can be caused by a number of factors, one of which can be an imbalance of chemicals in the brain. Medication is available that can treat this, and **just as you would see your doctor if you were physically ill, so it is equally important to consult him or her if you are seriously depressed**. But another cause of depression is often a perspective on life that emphasises failures rather than opportunities.

There is good evidence that a combination of medication **and** counselling is the most effective way to combat depression. The doctor may recommend a professional counsellor, or you can usually find a number listed in Yellow Pages, or with a web search. Professional counselling is likely to be the most effective method, but if this is impractical for whatever reason, there are approaches you can take yourself.

Four key stages of counselling

Counselling may sometimes be nothing more than talking about it all to a friend, partner or parent, who, after listening carefully to how life seems for you at the moment, and clarifying as much as possible, may be able to suggest a different perspective. For example, they could help you to look at the opportunities still open, instead of those closed; or suggest an alternative, perhaps more realistic set of goals if the first set has not been achieved. At times you may need to help friends who are feeling down; at other times your friends may be able to help you. The key stages of counselling for the sympathetic friend, partner or parent are:

1 Establish trust if you don't already have it – show that you really care, and will not just do this at odd times when you think about it.

2 Clarify. Encourage talk, even single words at first, if necessary, and then clarify in a positive, non-judgemental way, by restating what has been said, to make sure that you have understood it correctly. This needs active listening – make it very clear that you *are* listening. You may want to sit facing the person, with good eye contact, or you may find it easier to be at their side, perhaps while you are doing something simple enough not to distract you at all. You can even do this over the telephone or via email – some people find it easier to communicate over the phone or through email than by talking directly. Humour can help here, but be sensitive!

3 When you feel that you have a good understanding of what life looks like from the point of view of the other person, and not before, start to suggest alternative perspectives that fit the facts just as well. For example, focus on what *can* be done, rather than what cannot; the opportunities still open, rather than those closed; the person's success in getting as far as they did, rather than their not passing the final stage. Use a longer time frame in which it is possible to accomplish alternative goals, or to try different ways to achieve the same goal. Emphasise positive strengths rather than weaknesses, resources available – eg time – rather than those not available etc. Be very gradual about this, and expect to hear some vigorous denials at first. You are after all presenting an alternative view of life to one that has been in place for some time, and we are all scared of change. And don't argue. Your aim is to encourage a different perspective, not to force one.

4 Slowly if necessary, start to jointly pull out the consequences arising from this alternative, more positive perspective, which will probably include exploring some of the opportunities open, and re-addressing past events in a different way.

Most important are stages 1 and 2. If you simply stay at Stage 2, you will probably find that a new perspective starts to emerge even without your needing to suggest it.

Professional counselling is a very good alternative to this, but if for whatever reason this is not available or acceptable, the approach outlined above will almost certainly bring benefits, especially when used (where necessary) with prescribed antidepressant drugs (which usually take about one month before they start to have an effect).

But hopefully you will experience only the excitement that goes with a job search, just as with any activity which is important to you, and whose outcome is in doubt. Approached well, a job search can give a huge adrenaline rush, can change the course of your life, and be a positive experience that helps you to learn about yourself and clarify your real goals in life.

18
Head-hunters (executive search)

You may never need to employ a head-hunter yourself but, at some point in your career, if you have not already had a phone call from one, you will. And some organisations are now using student head-hunters to help them identify the really outstanding candidates at university, and persuade them to apply to their company. So it is useful to know how they operate, and why an employer might need to use their services.

Remember when I said earlier that looking through advertisements is not necessarily the best way to find the perfect job for you? Well, the same goes for organisations: in many cases advertisements or recruitment literature are not the most appropriate ways for them to find the top people for their jobs either. Why? Because the most talented are probably already in well paid jobs (or already have job offers), are performing well, are happy and fulfilled, and are not seriously looking at advertisements.

So what do you do if you are an organisation that wants the best person for the job? Well, you ask around to see who knows most about those employed in your line of business. These are the people who know who are the really good performers, irrespective of whether they are looking for a move or not. In many cases there are people in the organisation itself who know 'the field', ie who are the outstanding performers. But in some cases (for example a specialist job outside the main expertise of the organisation, or where internal rivalry makes it impractical) a head-hunter (they often prefer to call themselves executive search) may be asked to find the best candidate.

18.1 TYPES OF HEAD-HUNTERS

Almost unknown 40 years ago, there are now hundreds of head-hunting firms, ranging from individuals who work on their own (although sometimes with a network of associates), usually specialising in a particular area they are familiar with, to large firms with their own researchers, covering all areas and often providing global coverage.

The other general divide is between those firms that are pure head-hunters and those that provide a broader, less tailor-made approach, often including advertisements or web-based products as part of their offering. This second group (sometimes called executive selection) may be more appropriate when the job to be filled is more general, and there are likely to be a number of suitably qualified candidates. Fees for 'pure' head-hunters are seldom less than 33% of the first year's salary of the person recruited – so for senior jobs the fees can be considerable.

Student head-hunters who aim to identify the top talent at universities may be either fellow students who have already accepted a job offer from an organisation, and who have been asked to identify other talent; or alumni (previous students); or professional agencies specialising in university talent. Examples of the latter include *www.oxbridgelife.com*

18.2 THE HEAD-HUNTING PROCESS

In order to use head-hunting to its best advantage to you, either as a candidate or as a client (after all, at some stage you will be looking for staff), it helps to start with an understanding of the basic process. Head-hunting normally involves three broad stages, and two sets of people.

Identifying the client's needs

In the first stage the head-hunter gains a new client organisation who wants them to fill a specific job. They usually gain clients by networking or by recommendations from previous clients. If the head-hunter has already done some work for the client, he or she will usually be contacted by them again to fill a particular job.

After the client has agreed terms in writing, the head-hunter will spend time with the client identifying two main factors – the qualities and qualifications required for the job; and any candidates the client already knows about, or has in mind. It may seem strange that a client may know about candidates but still contract a head-hunter, but very often clients want to cast the net wider, and anyway are sometimes reluctant for a variety of reasons to approach the person themselves.

Research

The second stage involves the head-hunter's researcher or research team. Whereas the head-hunter is responsible for gaining new clients and keeping existing ones, as well as the overall direction of the search, the researcher has to identify a long list of possible candidates and then, after agreement with the client, approach them to see if they would be interested in the job. Some head-hunting firms have in-house research teams and resources, but there are a number of freelance researchers who are usually paid by the hour. Researchers often know as much if not more about the area they are researching than the head-hunter, but prefer not to have the bother of marketing themselves to clients. However, they earn much less.

A good researcher makes a huge difference to a search – she (it is usually she) has not only to assemble a list of potential candidates, but also to get past the various obstacles that organisations put in the way of people approaching their most valuable employees. Receptionists, switchboard operators and secretaries are common 'obstacles', so it is not unusual for researchers to phone potenial candidates after normal work hours, and to try to get hold of internal telephone directories so that they can dial the correct extension direct.

Short list

The third stage reverts to the head-hunter and the client, who consider what should be by this time a short list of only the top candidates, approach them for interview, select the best and make an offer. This is another part of the process where the head-hunter earns their substantial fee – persuading reluctant but very good candidates to come for interview, and to accept job offers when they are already in jobs that they are perfectly satisfied with.

The selection process is usually by interview – certainly candidates are very sensitive at this stage that their present employers do not become aware that they are considering alternatives (although it is not unheard of for some executives to deliberately allow this to be known, in order to secure a promotion or similar). However, the need for discretion does mean that any form of group assessment centre is out of the question. Some well-managed head-hunting firms do use a series of exercises that have all the validity of an assessment centre (for example a presentation, a discussion with client executives, etc) but without any candidate group work. Again for the sake of discretion, references are not normally taken up until a job offer is about to be made or has been made.

The head-hunter will usually see the shortlisted candidates, but this is not part of the formal selection process. The client is responsible for this.

18.3 WHEN SHOULD AN ORGANISATION USE A HEAD-HUNTER?

So, imagine you work for an organisation that's looking for a candidate, and you are responsible for finding the right person. How should you decide whether to use a head-hunter? Essentially, consider a head-hunter if you believe there is only a small number of people who could do the job, and they are unlikely to be looking for a move. If this is the case, and you think the fee of 33% of the selected candidate's first year's salary would be a good investment to get the right person, then choose your head-hunter with care.

Personal recommendations are best, and by this I don't just mean a recommendation of the overall firm; it has to be a recommendation of the individual. Head-hunters vary widely in quality and in their knowledge of particular areas of expertise, and you do not want to have someone assigned to you who knows little of your business area. This can be worse than useless, and no amount of 'guarantees' (see 18.4 below) will make up for the one or two years wasted. Many executives use the head-hunter who brought them to the firm in the first place. This is the best recommendation, I suppose, though it does risk a certain 'cronyism' that may eventually be resented.

If you don't have any good personal recommendation, there is an organisation called the Association of Executive Search Consultants to which almost all the best and most reputable organisations belong. See *www.aesc.org* They have a service that will help you identify suitable executive search firms.

If the fees for executive search cannot be justified, consider executive selection agencies, which focus on selecting from candidates who have responded to advertisements. Or look at sites like *www.goldjobs.com* which offer many of the advantages of search, at a fraction of the cost. Alternatively, set up your own search operation, and use the knowledge already in your organisation to identify and attract the best external candidates. You will probably require some expertise – a researcher at least – but it is perfectly practical and can literally save you millions. And you keep control of the information inside the organisation.

18.4 GUARANTEES

Most head-hunters provide a form of 'guarantee'. If the selected candidate does not perform well, or leaves the job within one year, then the head-hunter will do another search to find a replacement, at no cost to the client other than expenses. But be aware that the unsatisfactory recruit, together with the upset caused, will probably have cost the organisation far more than can be compensated by any guarantee. So whilst a guarantee is useful, it is by no means cost free.

18.5 HOW CAN HEAD-HUNTERS HELP YOU FIND A BETTER JOB?

So, is there any way that you, a job hunter, can use this well-established system to your advantage?

Well, the first opportunity comes when you are phoned, probably early in the morning or late in the evening, usually in the office, by someone who says that she is looking for an executive to fill a certain position, and that you have been recommended as someone who knows this area particularly well. Depending on how busy you are, this may be sufficient flattery to keep your interest. The caller will then briefly describe the job, and (usually) ask if you know anyone who might be suited to this job.

Note that she probably will not ask you outright if you would be interested – that can be left to you. It is much easier and safer for the researcher (the caller) not to ask you directly if you want the job. She may well be working for a competitor of your present employer, and if it gets known that they are 'poaching' staff, there may be retaliation in some form or another. So get as much information about the job as you can – consider it market research at the least. For example, if the pay is 30% more than you are currently getting, it is at least an indication that your market rate may be higher than you think. (But remember that at this stage the researcher may well be just compiling a long list, so do not go straight out and buy that new car.)

To move or not to move

If you are genuinely happy in your present job, and don't want to move even for the salary and whatever other benefits are offered, say so, and the researcher will probably end the conversation by asking you again if you know of anyone who would be suitable. This is an opportunity to do a favour for friends who you know are unhappy in their present job. But be fair, only recommend those who you think would be at least reasonable candidates. Do this a few times, and you will become known as a source, and are likely to develop a type of rapport with the caller and/or the head-hunter she is working for, so that when and if you **do** want a move, they will at least be interested, and you may find they have the contacts you need.

However, if you decide you **are** interested in the particular job mentioned by the researcher, then in addition to finding out all you can about the job, and the client organisation (the researcher may well be coy about this, and hide behind generalisations – 'a large company in a similar field to yours'; or simply, 'I am not able to tell you who the client is'), say that you might be interested, and see what happens. You may be asked if you have a current résumé (remember what I said about keeping your résumé up to date, even if you are not actively looking for another job?).

You may have some organisations that you definitely do not want your name to be forwarded to. For example, there have been cases where the researcher genuinely does not know the name of the client organisation, and approaches (mistakenly) people in the same organisation. This is embarrassing for everyone involved. Or you may know of a number of other organisations that you would not be prepared to work for – it is perfectly reasonable to state that you do not want your résumé to be sent to X, Y or Z organisations.

Thereafter, it is a matter of waiting (often far longer than you think), following the selection process, finding excuses for getting away to meet the new organisation, and if you are fortunate, negotiating a salary package and any other issues you need. For example, it may be necessary for you to take Friday afternoons off every other week to care for your child. Or you may want to ensure a transfer of pension rights, or a guarantee that you will have a secretary or whatever. All of these issues are best negotiated before you accept the position, not after.

And the package needs to be sufficient to make you prepared to take the risk of leaving your present employer, so it may well need to be worth more than what you consider to be your true 'market value'. At times a one-off joining bonus may be offered to get round this – ie to encourage you to join, without inflating salaries, or paying you more than others at a similar level in the organisation you are joining.

Making yourself known to head-hunters

If you have not been contacted by a head-hunter or their researcher, and want to be considered by them for some of these enticing jobs that are not advertised, but are filled by head-hunters, what can you do? Well, you can try identifying those head-hunters that specialise in your field of expertise (I have already mentioned the AESC *www.aesc.org* but a simple web search will probably identify most of them), and you can try sending a covering letter with your best résumé, but don't hold your breath.

It may just happen to arrive at a time when the researcher is looking to fill a job that you might be suitable for (or at least as a source), or it may be entered into a database, but be prepared for it to be binned, without even an acknowledgement. If it is entered into a database, do not think it will be kept for ever. Good researchers reckon only a résumé or information that is up to date to within the current 12 months is valid and can (more or less) be relied upon.

The better way to bring yourself to the attention of head-hunters is to network more, to write articles for any of the trade publications, or present papers at conferences or events. Not only will you gain the satisfaction of becoming known as an 'expert', you may well be increasing the market's awareness of you, and your own market value. If that's not what you want, and you are happy in your present employment, you have probably found the right job for you. Enjoy.

Appendix 1
Check-list of occupations, example salaries and number of vacancies

The main purpose of this table is to provide a check-list of possible jobs available. The salaries and vacancies are from *www.reed.co.uk*, and are given as an example of the information that is available. (Salaries relate to UK organisations and are averaged across the UK.) The jobs list in this table will do quite well for the USA, Australia, New Zealand, Canada, Europe, Asia, Africa, South America etc. For more focus and up-to-date salary and vacancy information, access a similar job site in the particular country you are interested in. Website details are given at the end of the table.

Jobs to consider	Approximate UK pay	Typical number of vacancies
Accounting (not qualified)		
Accounts admin.	£16,941	1,649
Assistant accountant	£20,637	1,530
Credit controller	£18,276	1,634
Graduate trainee	£18,345	79
Insolvency	£29,195	89
Ledger clerk	£16,578	1,537
Legal cashier	£20,288	212
Part qualified accountant	£26,341	1,437
Payroller	£20,562	768

Accounting (not qualified)	Approximate UK pay	Typical number of vacancies
Practice (non-qualified)	£22,950	529
Qualified by experience	£29,753	468
Other accountancy	£26,078	1,783

Accountant (qualified)	Average salary	No of vacancies
Analyst	£37,204	637
Auditor	£37,436	1,645
Company secretary	£37,229	11
Cost accountant	£36,403	35
Director	£68,280	106
Finance manager	£43,460	681
Financial accountant	£36,073	451
Financial consultant	£44,263	30
Financial controller	£46,714	498
Forensic accountant	£45,583	22
Insolvency	£53,924	66
Interim manager	£42,820	6
Life accountant	£50,000	5
Management accountant	£33,674	601
Newly qualified	£34,990	387
Practice manager	£45,025	221
Practice partner	£67,605	63
Project accountant	£40,394	77
Qualified by experience	£29,753	468

Syndicate accountant	£43,750	6
Systems accountant	£38,990	53
Tax accountant	£43,418	413
Trust accountant	£46,300	7
Other accountancy qualified	£39,012	702

Administrator and secretarial	Average salary	No of vacancies
Administrator	£16,326	4,871
Data entry clerk	£14,398	185
Facilities manager	£29,809	226
HR administrator	£17,968	437
Legal secretary	£19,209	2,787
Medical secretary	£18,238	39
Office clerk	£13,193	180
Office manager	£22,113	344
PA	£21,765	1,212
Receptionist	£14,541	1,022
Secretary	£18,131	1,098
Typist	£16,275	74
Other Admin and secretarial	£17,967	1,717

Banking	Average salary	No of vacancies
Analyst	£30,262	185
Back office	£18,634	95
Compliance	£41,947	132
Corp actions/divs	£48,381	18

Banking	Average salary	No of vacancies
Derivatives	£44,545	96
Equity	£48,009	36
Fixed income	£36,722	18
Fund administration	£27,189	74
Fund management	£46,708	47
FX/MM	£36,593	15
Private banking	£51,404	150
Project management	£46,529	51
Retail banking	£41,941	1,391
Risk/credit analyst	£36,734	169
Sales/traders	£28,290	113
Settlements	£31,724	39
Trade support	£31,776	32
Trainee	£31,541	169
Treasury	£37,063	26
Other banking	£34,647	877

Building services	Average salary	No of vacancies
Bricklayer	£25,400	10
Commercial	£35,436	272
Design	£31,636	690
Electrician	£27,259	58
Engineering	£31,765	570
Foreman	£29,898	49
Joiner	£25,033	23
Labourer	£16,745	6

Managerial	£41,724	850
Mechanical fitter	£23,296	8
Painter/Decorator	£20,667	4
Pipe fitter	£45,000	1
Planning	£39,712	178
Plasterer	£24,036	8
Plumber	£24,136	21
Quantity surveyor	£34,006	1,714
Supervisor	£32,235	79
Surveying	£34,504	744
Tiler	£32,250	2
Welder	£21,570	6
Other building and construction	£36,081	1,397
Other trades and labour	£25,991	46

Customer services	Average salary	No of vacancies
Account manager	£22,421	303
Contact centre manager	£29,671	273
Customer service adviser	£16,232	3,235
Customer services manager	£29,250	248
Team leader	£21,180	338
Other customer service	£18,694	1,335

Education	Average salary	No of vacancies
Adult education	£23,325	77
Assistant	£19,120	5
Further	£26,020	52
Higher	£28,198	6
Key Stage 1	£29,343	12
Key Stage 2	£31,287	16
Key Stage 3	£26,913	5
Key Stage 4	£45,500	1
Non-teaching	£24,542	26
Nursery	£19,511	104
NVQ assessor	£22,789	185
Primary	£24,782	25
Prisoner education	n/a	n/a
Secondary	£34,053	76
Special needs	£30,680	6
Supply teacher	£27,200	2
Other education	£22,857	145

Engineering	Average salary	No of vacancies
Aeronautical	£33,997	266
Automotive	£25,714	621
Building services	£32,212	900
Chemical/process	£34,656	133
Civil	£31,577	846
Electrical	£28,938	772
Electronic	£29,729	1,050

Field	£26,228	242
Geotechnical	£29,968	294
Maintenance	£26,680	847
Manufacturing	£26,595	757
Marine	£31,584	53
Materials	£30,309	61
Mechanical	£28,651	787
Project manager	£38,239	325
Structural	£34,559	350
Systems	£35,208	300
Other engineering	£28,750	1,770

Financial services	Average salary	No of vacancies
Actuarial	£48,920	259
Compliance	£32,273	496
Independent financial adviser	£46,982	2,918
Investments	£43,782	417
Mortgage adviser	£50,719	2,947
Mortgage underwriter	£25,204	233
Mortgages – other	£35,949	706
Paraplanner	£24,969	342
Pensions	£29,797	1,346
Retail financial adviser	£54,929	1,988
Sales support	£22,360	797
Other financial services	£32,439	2,107

General insurance	Average salary	No of vacancies
Account executive	£36,598	426
Account handler	£24,234	481
Actuarial	£54,013	34
Broker	£26,887	631
Claims	£22,719	722
Commercial	£29,879	734
Loss adjusting	£34,036	118
Personal lines	£20,609	472
Risk management	£37,787	127
Underwriting	£28,903	673
Other general insurance	£32,292	1,168

Health	Average salary	No of vacancies
Ambulance technician	£18,000	1
Art therapy	n/a	n/a
Carer	£14,733	46
Chiropody/podiatry	£60,000	1
Clinical psychology	£52,500	2
Counselling	£17,035	1
Dentistry	£67,317	373
Dietetics	n/a	n/a
Health education/promotion	£23,447	15
Health visitor	n/a	n/a
Midwifery	£35,000	1
Nursing	£24,241	157
Occupational therapy	£28,535	41

Optometry	£31,592	184
Orthotics/prosthetics	£24,000	1
Pharmacy	£36,371	66
Phlebotomy	n/a	n/a
Physiotherapy	£23,923	17
Psychotherapy	£25,000	2
Radiography/sonography	£27,448	53
Speech/language therapy	£30,000	5
Other health and medicine	£27,162	230

Hospitality and catering	Average salary	No of vacancies
Assistant manager	£18,041	504
Bar manager	£22,174	245
Barista	£12,394	11
Chef de partie	£16,272	589
Chef manager	£22,986	70
Commis-chef	£13,268	226
Events manager	£22,147	263
Head/executive chef	£27,542	268
Hotel manager	£27,385	281
Housekeeper	£16,994	149
Kitchen staff	£13,961	70
Pastry chef	£19,524	74
Receptionist	£15,094	457
Restaurant manager	£20,960	1,246
Sous-chef	£20,362	1,013
Waiting/bar staff	£13,440	255
Other hospitality and catering	£21,148	1,136

Human resources	Average salary	No of vacancies
Employee relations	£29,830	26
HR administrator	£17,968	437
HR adviser	£27,005	464
HR consultant	£36,511	110
HR director	£57,845	21
HR manager	£36,628	484
In-house recruiter	£27,890	105
Quality assurance	£26,486	17
Trainer	£24,977	286
Training manager	£32,928	191
Other HR and training	£30,676	474

IT	Average salary	No of vacancies
Analyst programmer/developer	£31,873	851
Business/systems analyst	£36,597	477
Consultant	£43,779	1,257
Database administrator	£29,838	180
Database developer	£31,879	142
Datacoms engineer	£30,770	50
Desktop support	£26,300	1,402
Helpdesk	£21,170	686
IT sales	£38,544	2,076
IT/systems manager	£42,202	1,210
Marketing	£31,206	132
Middleware	£55,375	13
Network analyst	£33,348	123

Network security	£38,668	105
Project manager	£42,074	668
Quality assurance	£30,417	84
Software developer	£32,244	2,159
Software engineer	£36,094	743
Systems testing	£34,661	203
Systems/network admin	£29,942	534
Technical author	£32,789	43
Technical trainer	£30,410	139
Telecoms engineer	£33,915	
Web design	£24,430	114
Web developer	£28,327	371
Other IT	£30,807	1,901

Legal	**Average salary**	
Company secretary	£20,941	23
Conveyancing	£28,289	348
In-house	£42,866	103
Law graduate	£43,479	48
Legal cashier	£20,288	212
Legal executive	£40,043	452
Legal secretary	£19,209	2,787
Paralegal	£32,501	565
Partner	£64,231	358
Partnership secretary	£22,250	12
Private practice	n/a	n/a
Solicitor	£46,401	2,290
Other legal	£30,084	1,253

Leisure and tourism	Average salary	No of vacancies
Airline	£28,920	14
Beauty and spa	£18,711	39
Business travel	£24,494	161
Health and fitness	£23,876	161
Reservations	£18,244	182
Sports coaching	£25,250	8
Travel agent and consultant	£19,944	129
Other leisure and tourism	£24,734	520

Manufacturing	Average salary	No of vacancies
Health and safety	£33,387	96
Manager	£35,343	335
Purchasing	£30,461	115
Quality control	£23,976	180
Semi-skilled operator	£16,305	68
Skilled operator	£19,248	123
Supervisor	£23,068	158
Other manufacturing	£24,005	468

Marketing and PR	Average salary	No of vacancies
Account executive	£20,952	233
Account manager	£29,569	522
Events manager	£24,652	123
Market research	£28,661	740
Marketing assistant	£19,341	290
Marketing director	£48,362	82

Marketing executive	£24,111	383
Marketing manager	£37,308	522
Public relations/publicity	£27,759	352
Other marketing and PR	£27,213	962

Other media/creative/design	Average salary	No of vacancies
Advertising	£25,873	186
Arts and entertainment	£32,935	12
Design agency	£27,568	124
Fashion design	£25,981	69
Freelance	£20,000	1
Graphic design	£23,835	170
Interior design	£26,764	47
New media	£32,238	193
Press	£23,061	39
Publishing	£25,686	213
Radio	£19,857	9
Television	£27,518	46
Other media, creative and design	£26,217	405

Public sector	Average salary	No of vacancies
Central government	£40,394	8
Development	£30,988	13
Environmental	£21,856	33
Housing	£24,575	118
Law enforcement	£23,167	7

Public sector	Average salary	No of vacancies
Libraries	£35,000	2
Local government	£33,190	20
Museums and galleries	£38,000	1
Planning	£32,754	21
Policy	£30,602	9
Probation/prison service	£28,894	4
Procurement	£35,753	4
Project management	£36,370	13
Public sector finance	£32,152	13
Regeneration	£41,150	5
Other public sector	£23,657	114

Recruitment	Average salary	No of vacancies
Account manager	£30,561	286
BD executive/manager	£41,556	144
Branch/recruitment manager	£37,755	976
Director	£65,364	37
Divisional/regional manager	£42,929	144
Graduate/trainee consultant	£25,897	1,330
On-site consultant	£26,146	104
Recruitment consultant	£29,826	9,037
Researcher/resourcer	£28,451	435
Search and selection consultant	£43,386	181
Senior recruitment consultant	£36,281	1,540
Team leader	£40,740	235
Other recruitment consultancy	£26,878	198

Retail	Average salary	No of vacancies
Area manager	£33,087	95
Asst manager	£17,559	769
Cashier	£15,520	28
Floor manager	£20,568	130
Merchandiser	£24,040	236
Purchasing	£32,791	156
Store manager	£22,187	1,284
Store staff	£15,651	409
Team leader	£15,790	131
Other retail	£21,386	618

Sales	Average salary	No of vacancies
Account manager	£28,859	1,712
Business development	£33,199	1,624
Estate agent	£30,708	1,762
Field sales	£31,419	1,564
Fundraiser	£23,968	29
Home working	£25,775	43
IT sales	£38,456	1,902
Media sales	£29,375	801
Medical sales	£31,285	451
Recruitment consultant	£33,495	1,626
Sales director	£52,775	124
Sales executive	£30,322	4,497
Sales manager	£37,495	1,589
Telesales	£22,317	2,428
Telesales – inbound only	£19,316	194
Other sales	£29,227	2,042

Science	Average salary	No of vacancies
Analytical chemistry	£23,008	103
Bioanalysis	£35,267	18
Bioinformatics	£39,625	5
Biotechnology	£31,586	39
Chemical engineering	£30,574	14
Chemistry	£29,187	58
Clinical data management	£26,243	59
Clinical research	£38,299	307
Environmental science	£29,203	220
Food science	£24,234	68
Forensic science	£18,000	1
Formulation	£30,233	15
Inorganic chemistry	£25,000	2
Laboratory technician	£20,370	79
Life science	£31,604	23
Materials science	£27,172	23
Medical devices	£34,297	30
Medical information/writing	£36,670	66
Microbiology	£20,561	29
Organic chemistry	£30,750	8
Physics	£34,979	92
Polymer chemistry	£26,500	26
Process chemistry	£24,000	12
Quality assurance	£26,347	67
Quality control	£24,574	72
Regulatory affairs	£36,268	82
Researcher	£26,312	18
Sales	£30,098	204

SAS programming	£56,667	5
Statistics	£34,625	26
Validation	£29,800	11
Other scientific	£29,667	324

Social care	Average salary	No of vacancies
Advice worker	£21,136	4
Care assistant	£14,346	35
Care manager	£28,476	263
Case worker	£23,591	6
Child care/nanny	£19,083	141
Project worker	£25,248	18
Qualified social worker	£34,733	96
Residential social worker	£20,388	8
Social work assistant	£27,667	3
Support worker	£17,528	55
Youth worker	£26,593	3
Other social care	£27,268	98

Transport and logistics	Average salary	No of vacancies
Airline	£25,611	25
Driving	£18,373	150
Loader/shifter	£15,162	13
Logistics	£26,467	401
Picker/packer	£14,787	17
Postal worker	£16,831	8
Rail	£37,358	94
Shipping	£22,596	601

Transport and logistics	Average salary	No of vacancies
Supply chain	£27,668	120
Team leader	£22,324	46
Transport planner	£20,819	98
Warehouse operative	£14,651	105
Warehouse supervisor	£23,879	113
Other transport and logistics	£23,859	663

Other	Average salary	
Agriculture	£19,875	
Archivist/curator	n/a	
Cleaner	£16,146	
Clergy	n/a	
Conservation/environment	£28,091	
Economist/statistician/business analyst	£32,707	
Facilities manager	£29,809	
Gardener	£16,533	
Home working	£25,775	
Hospital porter	£20,850	
Housekeeper/caretaker	£16,534	
Management consultant	£33,588	
Pest control	£27,500	
Political researcher	£17,750	
Project manager	£31,845	
Quality assurance	£24,299	
Security	£21,301	
Senior management	£41,291	

Textiles	£24,928	
Translator/interpreter	£19,056	
Undertaker	£21,748	
Uniformed services	£17,327	
Veterinary services/animal care	£19,694	
Source: www.reed.co.uk Other sites are also good, eg *monster.co.uk* or *monster.com* or *hays.co.uk*	Average salary is average of all vacancies posted on the *reed.co.uk* site.	Vacancies are those shown on the site at the time.

For the latest data go to the specific websites, eg *www.reed.co.uk*

Appendix 2
Sample table prepared by a job seeker to identify underlying motivators

This sample table has been prepared using the method described in Chapter 3, Exercise 6, to identify the job seeker's underlying motivators and jobs that are most likely to meet them. The underlying motivators are shown as A–E and defined at the bottom of the table. The ratings the job seeker gave to each are given on a scale of 0–5. The jobs were taken from the list in Appendix 1. This is a powerful method to identify what motivates you, and the type of jobs that are most likely to keep you interested and stimulated.

Job	Average pay	Vacancies	Criteria:					Sum	Comment
			A	B	C	D	E		
Corporate actions/divs	£48,381 pa	18	5	4	5	5	3	22	M&A
Law graduate	£43,479 pa	48	4	5	4	5	4	22	Business law
Insolvency	£53,924 pa	66	4	4	5	4	4	21	Big four practice
Uniformed services	£17,327 pa		4	3	5	3	5	20	Army, navy, CG etc
FX/MM (foreign exchange)	£36,593 pa	15	5	5	4	5	1	20	Trader
Project management	£36,370 pa	13	5	2	5	5	3	20	SS

Newly qualified accountant	£34,990 pa	387	4	4	3	4	4	19	Big four firm
Law enforcement	£23,167 pa	7	4	3	5	3	4	19	Police
Retail manager	£35,343 pa	335	3	4	4	4	4	19	Graduate trainee
Electronic engineer	£29,729 pa	1,050	3	3	4	4	4	18	Design engineer
Independent financial adviser	£46,982 pa	2,918	3	4	4	4	3	18	Lots of client contact
Central government	£40,394 pa	8	4	2	3	3	5	17	Exposure, but pay?
Compliance	£41,947 pa	132	3	3	3	3	3	15	
Underwriting	£28,903 pa	673	2	3	4	3	3	15	Insurance
Equity	£48,009 pa	36	4	5	1	3	1	14	Equity researcher
Retail banking in an international banking group	£41,941 pa	1,391	3	3	2	2	4	14	
HR adviser	£27,005 pa	464	2	3	2	2	5	14	

Criteria	Rating
A = exclusivity/high status organisation	5 = lots/top 20%
B = Pay (top 20%) – above that less important	4 = well above average
C = changing environment with clear deliverables	3 = average for this criteria
D = small high-powered teams, with good motivation.	2 = below average
E = good promotion prospects to manage these teams	1 = lowest 20%

Appendix 3
Accuracy of selection methods in predicting job performance

This table shows how accurate the various selection methods are in predicting subsequence job performance. The methods are shown in the right-hand column, from the most accurate at the top to the least accurate at the bottom. A correlation of 1.0 indicates perfect prediction, a correlation of 0 indicates no accuracy at all – the selector would have done as well to have employed people at random.

These results are taken from a meta-anaylsis which combines a very large number of studies to come up with a reliable estimate of the accuracy of the different selection methods.

Correlation	
1.0 Perfect prediction	
0.9	
0.8	
0.7	Assessment centres (0.68)
0.6	
0.5	Work samples (0.54) Ability tests (0.54)
0.4	Structured interviews (0.44)
0.3	Personality tests (0.38) Unstructured interviews (0.33)
0.2	
0.1	References (0.13)
0.0 (No accuracy)	Astrology, graphology (0.0)

Source: Anderson, N and Cunningham-Snell, N (2000), 'Personnel Selection'. In Chmiel N (ed), *Introduction to Work and Organisational Psychology: A European Perspective.* Oxford: Blackwell.

Appendix 4a
Example résumé with some work experience

The names and some details have been changed in this and subsequent résumés, but they are all real people and real résumés.

The résumés have expanded to fit the format of this book. A two page résumé may appear as three pages here, or a three page résumé may appear as four or five pages, but they illustrate some of the content and formatting you can choose.

PAT SMITH

Home Address: 3 Fulton Street, Southampton,
Hampshire, MA13 1VX
Mobile: 087932590271
E-mail: patsmith84@aaaaaa.com
Birth Date: 17.05.84
Nationality: British

EDUCATION

2002–2005 Plymouth University, B.A. Management (Honours 2:2)

International Marketing, (1st class) Sustainable Tourism, (1st class), Event Planning, Strategy for business, Law (contract and health & safety), Financial planning and reporting, Outdoor Recreation Issues, Marketing.

All modules successfully passed with at least a 2:2 grade.

Dissertation: Marketing Consultancy for a large Leisure Centre, I analysed current users and potential target customer base in the area, identified needs, preferences, brand loyalties, barriers to attending, also competitors and costs.

A levels: Geography (C), Economics (D); A/S: Information Technology (C)

GCSEs: Mathematics (A), English Language (B), English Literature (B), Physics (C), Chemistry (C), Biology (C), Geography (B), French (B), Design Technology (D)

EMPLOYMENT

Oct 2005–date Seaborne Agency

Responsible for assessing equivalency of competencies for a wide variety of foreign certificates of water borne competency, contacting the relevant authorities, corporations and the individuals to confirm when necessary, and collecting and enforcing payment.

2005 Corporate Events – Cruiser; Cyclone Racing; Panther Powerboating

Leading and instructing senior clients and executives on corporate hospitality events.

2004–date Instructor and Administrator, The Moorings Water Activity Centre.

M.W.A.C. is one of the major Leisure/Outdoor Activities Centres in the UK, with 80+ staff. Income from these courses can be as high as £10,000/week. As Instructor for sailing and power boating I am often called on to be the Senior

Instructor responsible for up to 30 people and 5 other instructors including full responsibility for organisation and safety in this potentially life threatening environment. *I regularly receive the highest level of feedback from participants for this course*. Trainees range from corporate executives on team building exercises or away-days, to children, ages 6–60 and abilities from athlete to special needs, disadvantaged and disabled, always a challenge in the sailing/power-boating environment – but a specially satisfying one. Planning, coordinating, and managing are significant roles within my job. Safety is paramount and a thorough understanding of risk-assessments, the AALA (Adventure Authorities Licensing Authority) guidelines, COSHH and RIDDOR. I run this job concurrently with Seaborne.

Jan 2003–Nov 2003 Supervisor, Front of House, The Place Nightclub

I was responsible for motivating and controlling the bar staff, collecting the cash floats for all of the eight tills (up to 20,000 pounds/night in total), checking the amounts and setting up the area. At the end of the night I cashed up, compiled reports and sent the night's figures to the head office. This provided funding for my University degree.

2002–2003 Lifeguard/Recreation Assistant: The Moorings Complex

Although principally a lifeguard, my duties included maintenance of the building and all safety equipment. I was responsible for ensuring application of the safety regulations and procedures, as well as customer service. I was a full member of the team, attended staff training every month and renewed my National Pool Lifeguard Qualification every two years. I had to have a precise understanding of the COSHH, RIDDOR and Health and Safety at Work regulations concerning the chemicals and equipment in the building.

2001–2002 Lifeguard, Recreation Assistant, and Instructor, Battery Leisure

I was a lifeguard, and also gave a substantial amount of Assistant Swimming Instruction, teaching both adults and children from in the water and on the side of the pool. I both assisted and ran classes by myself including lessons for intermediate swimmers.

QUALIFICATIONS, INTERESTS AND OTHER EXPERIENCE

Qualifications: I hold a RYA Dinghy Instructor qualification with a keelboat endorsement and have completed the Senior dinghy instructor course. Passed RYA Day skipper theory course (to be in charge of larger yachts) and RYA first aid certificate. RYA qualified powerboat instructor and RYA qualified safety boat driver. I have the International Certificate of Competence and completed the advanced powerboat driver course in October. I also hold a VHF licence and have a full, clean driving licence.

Borneo Expedition: While still at school, I spent a month on expedition in Borneo with Project Drake. I had to raise £3,850 through group and individual fund raising activities and events. In Borneo, I was responsible for arranging the accommodation (from Kuching) for the entire group aged 16–18 in Bintulu; also travel and food arrangements.

Kenya: Between finishing my A-Levels and starting university in 2000, I spent three months living and working in Kenya teaching a range of subjects in a boarding school. I was teaching in an English speaking boarding school on the outskirts of Nairobi. It was necessary to fully integrate into the Kenyan culture and way of life, adhering to their customs and traditions.

Sails for Cancer: I prepared an event for Sails for Cancer.

REFERENCES Available on request.

Appendix 4b
Example undergraduate résumé

Julia Simmons

Address: 67 High Street, Manchester MA2 3RA
Mobile: 07757 444113
Email: mail@aaaaaa.com
Date of Birth: 14 September 1983
Nationality: British

Education

University of Manchester

- School of Management: BSc (Hons) Business Administration (2002–2006)
- Four year course including 2 six month full time periods of employment in major organisations
- Results to date (and predicted degree) – Good 2:1
- Modules include Accounting, Strategic Analysis, Organisational Behaviour, Financial Markets, Investment Banking, European Business, French, Business Law, Technology and Innovation Management, Financial Regulation.

Midhurst School (1996–2001)

A Levels: Business (A), Chemistry (A), Physics (B), German (B)

GCSEs: 3 A*, 5 A, 2 B

Work Experience

Northern Financial Derivatives Exchange – Analyst
Feb 2005–August 2005

- Responsible for Analysis & Product Development in the Financial Derivatives Product Management Team
- A full member of the team (4 Product Managers, 3 Marketing Managers) responsible for promoting and managing all financial derivative products on the exchange, including standing in for Product Managers
- I analysed new product launches for Directors, daily market reports for the CEO, analysed the bond market, and created and distributed General Notices which are sent to all members of the exchange, including gaining legal clearances for these public documents.

- I prepared the formal proposal to Directors for a new financial derivative product, with estimates of market size, potential revenues, profits, and risk
- I led the tender process for Market Making (creation of a market – encouraging trading firms to enhance the liquidity of one of our financial derivatives), including invitations to bid, stringent legal considerations, evaluation criteria, performance related payments. This produced savings of £500,000/year.

Pacific Bank – Project Manager July 2003–January 2004

- Project manager on Project Hermes. This involved 100+ people full time in the transferral of all credit card transactions for the whole group from a third party data provider to an in-house system
- A high profile technical and business project, it required me to rapidly learn the relevant business knowledge as well as the required IT/IS skills
- I quickly became a core member of the data mapping team, and then graduated to more proactive roles, eg leading the 'issue solving' teleconference calls with the US side of the operation
- I set up 'mocks', full simulations of the new system over weekends. These had the potential for major disruption to customers and required detailed preparation and close management

Territorial Army – Signals Unit (about 30 days/year)
October 2002–July 2005

- Passed selection, basic training and accepted into B Company (Manchester Signals Unit)
- Extensive training for military and disaster situations (civil contingency reaction force) including deployment to Georgia (Eastern Europe) in July 2004 to train the Georgian army.

Social Services Youth Offending Team – Juvenile Offender Representative September 2002–Present

- I am on call evenings and weekends to support and represent young people who are in police custody.

Combined Utilities – Field Sales August 2001–November 2001

- Responsible for direct selling of Combined Utilities products to customers
- Set up exhibition stands and targeted members of the public to use our services

- Role required a sensitive, customer specific approach as well as a sense of humour
- Success reflected in weekly earnings well above targets (eg earnings in one week in excess of £1000)

Simmons Communications – Sole trader (and creator)
July 1999– March 2000

- When I was 17, I set up my own internet company as sole trader to exploit the significant price differential between high street stores and bulk distributors in electronic equipment.
- This involved procuring from distributors, advertising via search engine banners and in specialist magazines to attract customers. I achieved turnover of £20,000/year, profit £1000/year.
- I personally designed the website, set up a merchant account with Barclays and integrated the credit card facility into the online website

Manchester University Projects

My course involves many team projects based on real business situations, in addition to full time placements: eg

IT: Team Leader investigating how IT contributes to the success of Tesco

Finance: Carried out an investigation into the feasibility of a new set of financial reporting standards

Accounting: Analysed Debenhams Accounts to determine acquisition potential

Portfolio Project: Analysis into the commercial decline of a leading retailer

Action Project: Researched, planned and launched a commercial product in Hull

Activites, Interests and Achievement

- Achieved Duke of Edinburgh Award – Bronze, Silver and Gold
- Two Atlantic crossings on a 41ft yacht as watch leader
- National Electronics Prize – Young Electronic Designer Award (YEDA): 5th in National Finals, designing and building an original electronic appliance and then preparing a marketing plan (July 2000).

- Sub Aqua: Qualified as BSAC Sports Diver and completed 100+ open water dives.
- Karate: Achieved 7th Kyu / Orange Belt (March 2003).

Other Skills

- **Microsoft Word & Excel**: Advanced inc functions such as pivot tables & vlookup
- **Microsoft PowerPoint**: Prepared and given PP presentations to Senior Managers
- **General IT**: Fully competent with all PCs, including building my own computer
- **Website Design**: Proficient in MS FrontPage, Netobjects Fusion and static HTML
- **French**: Intermediate level (GCSE A*, University module 2:1 level)
- **German**: A level (B grade)

Gap Year (2001/2)

- **June – July**: Six week environmental assessment of coral reefs in Fiji.
- **August – November**: British Gas field sales – see work experience
- **November – December**: Atlantic Crossing from Canary Islands to St Lucia.
- **January – March**: Backpacking expedition with a friend – Cuba, Dominica,
- **April**: Sabah and Sarawak [North Borneo] including ascent of Mt Kinabalu [highest mountain in SE Asia].
- **May – June**: Atlantic Crossing from Florida to Azores via Bermuda.
- **June – August**: Worked in Sainsbury's Night Shift to finance my gap year.

References

Anthony Peters, Director UK Financial Derivatives

Tim Allan, Manager Pacific Bank

Harold Long, Manchester University Tutor

Appendix 4c
Example graduate résumé (completing Master's)

Laura M. Bennet

Oudezijds Achterburgwal 115 * 1012 DT Amsterdam, The Netherlands *
laurabenn@aaaaaaa.net
+31 (0) 616 202 6794

Education

Universiteit Van Amsterdam Law School, *L.L.M. International and European Law Specialising in International Law*

Expected Graduation: August 2006

- *Specialisations*: International Humanitarian Law, the Law of Military Operations, and International Refugee Law
- *Winner 'Best Oralist' of Dutch National Rounds, Member Dutch National Team*: Jessup International Law Competition 2006
- *Member, Jury Panel Judging 'Best Oralist'*: Telders International Law Competition 2006
- *Founder*: The Netherlands International Law and International Policy Forum for Young International Students and Professionals
- *Member*: International Law Faculty Student Council
- *Participant*: From Peace to Justice Conference 2006 – Beyond the Charter: Peace Security and the Role of Justice
- *Participant*: American Society of International Law Annual Conference
- *Participant*: Law of Refugee Status, Refugee Studies Centre, Oxford University

University of St Andrews *M.A. (Honours) in Politics* Graduated: June 2005

- *Specialisations:* International Law, specifically International Trade and Environmental Law, African and Middle Eastern Politics
- *Dissertation:* A comparison of American foreign policy in the Philippines and the lessons that could have been applied from that to the situation in Iraq
- *Member Scottish National Team:* Telders International Law Competition 2005

- *Co-Founder and Vice-President*: University of St Andrews Model International Court of Justice
- *Director:* 1200-person Harvard World Model United Nations Conference
- *Member:* St Andrews University Team-Racing Sailing Team

Brunel School, Bristol *International Baccalaureate* Graduated: May 2001

- *40 points*: International Baccalaureate (equivalent to AAAB at A-level – The Times 2001)
- *Distinction*: Institute of Linguists French Diploma
- *4 A*, 6 A*: UK General Certificate of Secondary Education

Work Experience

Somalia Project, *Netherlands/Somalia* April 2006–current

Assistant Coordinator

International development project building international legal competence in, at present, the Somalian Ministry of Justice, the Somali Parliament and the Somalian Civil Service College. I prepare background documentation, and manage day-to-day running of project.

Prof. Dr. Boules, *Universiteit van Amsterdam, Netherlands*

October 2005–June 2006

Research Assistant

Revising book for a second edition: *Free Movement of Persons within the European Community* (Kluwer Law, 2002). I prepared conference papers and drafted articles for publication.

Fortune Hilton, *Edinburgh, UK* February 2005–August 2005

Intern

I analysed the impact of upcoming developments in the Scottish political arena for this multinational lobbyist firm both for current clients and in order to target new clients more effectively. I prepared political briefs on Scottish Politics and monitored Scottish legislation.

Spirited Computing, *Edinburgh/London, UK*
April 2004–August 2004 and June 2003–August 2003

Recruitment Analyst

I invented and implemented a project to specialise new business strategy in selling IT contractors to the idiosyncrasies of the Scottish recruitment market. Resourcing for 'Key Accounts' team working with Bank of Scotland, Bacardi and PriceWaterhouse Coopers.

Paramount Capital, *Santiago de Chile, Chile* May 2002–September 2002

Researcher and Analyst

I prepared an investment and export study involving: examination of investment opportunities; product sourcing, liaison with producers, transporters, package design, backers and relevant government and embassy economic departments.

Short Internships/Positions, *London, UK* 1999–2001

British Fulbright Scholars Association – Office Manager (*3 months*); YTK Construction – Marketing and Development Intern (*4 months*); Sherborne-in-Southwark – Inner City Regeneration (*1 month*); Merrill Lynch Investment Bank (*Summer*); IMP Advertising (*Summer*).

Languages

English (native speaker); Advanced Spanish and French; Basic Dutch; Comprehension in Italian

Interests

Travel, Gastronomy, Sailing, Tennis, Music, Politics and Current Affairs

Appendix 4d
Example American-style résumé – university undergraduate

BART M. JONES

Bartjones@aaaa.com

College Address:	Home Address:
1768 Wesley Road	2580 Kirk Field
Denver, CO 80733	Redburn, CA 50575
(303) 369-8921	(813) 432-9567

Objective

A starting level position in a growing organisation that will use and develop my computing skills, enable me to contribute to the business and develop professionally.

Education

Denver State University

Major: Business Computing Science

Minor: Telecommunications

Expected Graduation: 2007; GPA to date: 3.2/4.0

Sample Courses

Introduction to Business Computing; Integrated Business Systems; Database Design; Computer Aided Design; Software Development Principles; Accounting; Introduction to Copyright and Patent Law; Software Development Tools; Project Management; Japanese Business Practices; Telecommunications; New Media Applications.

Nettlestead High School, CA, GPA 3.65/4.00

Work Experience:

May 2005–August 2005: Internship, Rathbone Industrial Filters Inc, CA, Computer Programmer/Analyst providing technical support for a team of 100 users, and troubleshooting. Assisted in preparations for a software upgrade and was on site over the weekend during implementation and testing.

June 2003–September 2003: Retail Assistant at ComputersRUs Store, assisting customers with decisions on computer and related electronic hardware and software.

January 2002–August 2002: Assistant at The Break Pizza House, waited tables, part-time cashier.

Competencies

Most Microsoft Applications; C/C++; and some networking packages

Skilled in diagnosing business problems into suitable computing terms.

Scholarships and Honors

Denver State University Faculty Scholarship

Member University Skiing Team (Slalom) and trained with the State Skiing Team

Awarded 'Entrepreneur of the Year' at school for a prototype personal security alarm system to minimise theft of mobile phones.

References

Available on request.

Appendix 4e
Example résumé with work experience and NGO objective

EDWARD P. ALBRIGHT

Born: 14 January 1971
14 The Highway
Sheffield
SN23 BR
UK
Telephone: 01623-459876, 0778-659-4134(m)
email: edwardpalbright@aaaaa.com

Profile: A communicator, advocate and writer with proven networking abilities, and awards from US and UK institutions, I am seeking a demanding position in a NGO. As a barrister I split my practice equally between advisory work and advocacy, delivering results under pressure and to tight deadlines. I have taught university courses and teamwork sessions including effective communication and language skills. I am committed to social justice, to enhancing the quality of life of disadvantaged people, and to assisting others to engage in activities that improve their lives. I have a particular commitment to environmental issues and sustainable development, to working for legal reform, and to working against all types of discrimination and injustice.

Education & Qualifications:

2005: TEFL qualification, TEFL Training, Cambridge

2002–2003: Pupillage at Matrix Chambers, Sheffield

2000–2002: Derby Law School

2001–PgDL (Postgraduate Diploma in Law)

2002–Bar Vocational Course

1996–2000: Leicester University

Ph.D. in Cultural Studies (Ethnography & Film Studies) For my Ph.D. case study I conducted a lot of interviews and other qualitative research; the body of my thesis required a comprehensive analysis of ethnographic theory and methodology.

1994–1996: University of Idaho: MA in Communication Studies

1991–1994: University of Glasgow (Second Year Entry)

MA (First Class Hons) Mental Philosophy

I studied Church History, English Literature, History, Linguistics, and Film Studies as well as Philosophy. I was secretary and then president of the Philosophy Society.

1991: Durban University, Tennessee, USA

1990: Faraday Community College, Tennessee USA

Art, American Literature, Classics, Creative Writing, English Literature & History, Physics and Philosophy (4.0 Grade Point Average).

1983–1990: Roehampton Grammar School:

O level (1987) Religious Studies (C); **GCSEs** (1988) in Art & Design (A); Economics (A); English Language (A); English Literature (A); French (B); History (A); Mathematics (B); Physics (B).

A levels (1990) English Literature (A plus Merit in Special Paper); History (B); Philosophy (A), Art (D);

Awards and Scholarships:

2001 – Queen Mother Scholarship, The Honourable Society of the Middle Temple

2000 – Diplock Scholarship, The Honourable Society of the Middle Temple

1996 – Three year doctoral research Scholarship from the British Academy

1992 – University of Glasgow Prize in Mental Philosophy (Moral Philosophy)

1990 – 1991: English-Speaking Union Scholarship

Employment history:

April 2003–date: Barrister. I am a junior tenant at Matrix Chambers, Sheffield. My practice is exclusively in Chancery and Commercial law, with emphases on housing, unmarried property disputes, civil injunctions, insolvency, and contractual disputes. I advise local government on policy as well as legal issues, and give training seminars at local authorities and private law firms.

2000–2002: While at law school I volunteered regularly at the Derby Child Contact Centre. I spent at least two days per month at the centre at weekends, supervising and facilitating contact between children and their parents, as well as managing situations between estranged parents.

1997–1999 & 2000: Regular Visiting Lecturer, Leicester University.

I created and taught courses on the Film & Literature BA, team-taught Film Studies BA courses and supervised Third Year dissertations. I also taught evening classes at the Sounding Board whilst I was at law school.

1994–1996 and Fall 1999: Lecturer, Communications Department, University of Idaho.

I created and ran courses to enable students to read, write, speak and think critically. I used a wide range of texts – from writings on the philosophy of religion to advertising campaigns to films and critical analyses of TV. Throughout my courses I focused on raising student awareness of issues of race, class, gender, sexuality and disability, and how language impacts perceptions of 'normality'.

Summer 1993: Tutor in Philosophy, University of Glasgow ACCESS course.

This was the first time the university allowed an undergraduate student to participate in teaching. I tutored groups of disadvantaged and/or under-achieving students in moral and political philosophy and I graded essays.

<u>Languages:</u>

- Spanish (Latin American) – good conversational standard; better at writing due to my translation work and need to correspond in Spanish;
- French – basic.

<u>IT Skills:</u>

- Experienced in Microsoft Office Suite applications and in using a range of internet browsers for research and communication.

Volunteer work, Hobbies and Interests:

I volunteered for a biodiversity survey with the local NGO-led youth group in Amarla, Botswana, and promoted eco-tourism development with members of the community and its councillors. I returned to Botswana to set up a furniture training project for villagers and am currently liaising with a range of government departments to obtain support and funding for the project, drafting and editing funding proposals, and preparing further income-generating activities for community projects. I also do conservation work with a group of other volunteers in locations across the UK, often learning new skills, eg dry-stone walling; also cinema, theatre, ballet and modern dance and martial arts – primarily tae kwon do and karate.

References:

Name	Contact details	Position
Dr Simon Jenkins	Communications Department University of Idaho Idaho City, ID 54987, USA Tel: +1 567 458 0181/0178 Email: sjenkins@ aaaaaaa.edu	Associate Professor and Leader in the Professional Development Programme.
Dr Ashley Mason	School of Cultural Studies Leicester University, LE11 6UZ Tel: +44 (0)123 776 6593 Email: amason@aaaaaaa. co.uk	Course Leader, Film Studies
Ms Patricia Green Mr Anthony Quilt	Matrix Chambers, Wilmslow Square Sheffield SH1 6MN Tel: +44 (0)542 674 8893 Email:green@aaaaaaaaa. co.uk quilt@aaaaaaaaa.co.uk	Barristers, Recorders, my Pupil Supervisors 2002–2003

Appendix 4f
Example cover letter applying to a vacancy

Recruitment Department
Wizard Electronics
123 Merchant Way
Northfield, NF34 8JP

13 Johnstone Rd
Tearside
Wyslow WU12 4PY
07855-730521
samerwin@aaaaaaa,com

3rd January 2007

APPLICATION FOR TELECOMMUNICATIONS PROJECT ENGINEER VACANCY ADVERTISED IN NEW SCIENTIST 1st JANUARY 2007

Please accept this letter and the attached résumé as my application for this position. I think you will find that my experience and background fit the requirements you identified. I have been keen to work for your organisation for some years, and believe that this vacancy is the right fit.

You required a degree in Telecommunications and significant engineering and commercial experience, including contact with customers. As you will see from my résumé, I have a Master's degree in Telecommunications, and my dissertation was on the economics of Mobile Telephony. I have six years' hands on experience in this field including ABC Telecomms, where I was in the western team installing new mobile towers. I was responsible for the detailed final design and supervising the contracts for ten of these. This required extensive consultation and negotiations with local councils and land owners, and keen attention to design, planning and costs during the actual construction. All the towers

I was responsible for were constructed on time and within budget. After three years I received an offer from Sunrise Mobiles to be deputy head of a team preparing a bid to provide mobile telephony to a small African state. I visited the country four times, and held discussions and negotiations with ministers. I drafted 80% of our bid, which was approved by the Board as 'very professional', and accepted as technically excellent by the Government's own consultants, but the Ministry decided to accept a bid from a rival firm. My firm is keen to retain my services, but I wish to move to your part of the country for personal reasons, hence this application.

I am very keen to meet you to explain in more detail what I have done and why I believe I would be the right person for this job. I can attend interviews at most times during June, but not from 24th–28th January. My present employer is not aware that I am applying to you, so please treat this application in confidence. I can be contacted by phone or my personal email. I would be grateful for your response before the end of January.

Yours,

Sam Erwin.

Att: Résumé

Covering letters should almost always be on a single page. This example was on a single page, but the formatting in this book has expanded it to two pages.

Appendix 5a
Example résumé with more experience – date and employment history format

This is the more usual format. See Appendix 5b for the same résumé formatted in terms of competencies.

The résumés have expanded to fit the format of this book. A two page résumé may appear as three pages here, or a three page résumé may appear as four or five pages, but they illustrate some of the content and formatting you can choose.

Douglas Campbell B.Eng. ACCA, MBA.

Business integration and change management

Home phone: 01365-497251
Email: douglh@aaaaaa.com
Mobile: 07684-332779

74 Aylesbury St
WINDSOR
Berkshire SL36 4XX

PROFILE

I am seeking further strategic change management opportunities at senior management level in high tech business development or corporate restructuring.

An experienced Production controller, business analyst and change project manager, I have eight years' offshore projects engineering in UK plus 12 years' experience with international corporations in IT, telecommunications, and distribution, including six years in the Middle and Far East. My specialist skills include project planning and management, financial forecasting and control, business systems integration and corporate restructuring in multicultural management settings.

I am a keen team player: innovative, analytical, versatile trouble-shooter, calm, adaptable, stimulated by periods of crisis or rapid change. I aim to be a catalyst for change, winning co-operation rather than demanding it.

EMPLOYMENT HISTORY

3/2002–date **Project Planning Director**, *Incubin Telecommunications*, London.

I prepared the investment analysis, proposals and presentations for major projects eg for a £75m overseas communications centre, office relocation and offshore support contracts, all of which were successfully implemented within budget and on time. I lead a team of up to 50 staff. I am responsible for HR and public relations roles in two smaller subsidiaries including government and media contacts.

5/98–2/2002 **Corporate Strategy and Contingency Planning Manager**, *Glow-worm Systems*, Slough, Industrial heating control systems.

I upgraded the contingency planning and ran rehearsals for major risks eg Y2K compliance project and international Intranet projects. I was responsible in the senior management team for strategic plans for internally and externally generated organisation change programmes to make us more responsive to the market. I developed and implemented financial policies and procedures associated with corporate changes, eg merger and de-merger. I provided induction and strategic guidance for new CEO and Boards of recently acquired subsidiaries. I was a facilitator for change management training and projects with direct input to short term restructuring and longer term company culture change projects.

1/90–3/98 **Project Manager, Business Integration (SAP)**, *Wong Enterprises*, Singapore and Hong Kong, IT component manufacturing.

I planned, selected and implemented a new logistics database, and planned the transitions to fully integrated business systems (purchasing, production and distribution etc) using SAP and transition management methodologies. I developed pre- and post-merger financing structures and directed subsidiaries in the UK and the Far East, building co-operation between local staff and senior management.

7/85–11/89 **Business Analyst (Overseas Ventures)**, *NingTel Europe Ltd*, London based + assignments in Egypt, Turkey and Spain.

I developed forecasting systems and co-ordinated contract and investment schedules to ensure self-financing growth through positive cash flows (up to £7.5m). I reviewed the organisation and management structures to identify opportunities for improved efficiency and co-operation plus updating to meet changing markets and business plans, saving $1 million/year.

12/83–6/85 **Offshore Projects Accountant**, *Belltec Engineering*, Aberdeen.

I was responsible for the financial planning for major projects up to £430 million, including financing sources during rapid growth. This included the introduction of management systems – from concept to commissioning, eg *Oracle* and *Synthafin v.3*. I established internal financial controls and external compliance including state, European and US regulations and ISO 9000 certification. I shared responsibility for all aspects of legal compliance drawing on specialist advice from Head Office advisers and external professional advisers. I ensured compliance with currency regulations.

10/79–12/83 **Trainee Project Engineer**, *Belltec Engineering*, Aberdeen. Sub-sea modules.

I led a team of 30 contractors, ensuring they were working to quality standards and the projects were successfully completed on time and meeting health and safety targets. My operating budget was £15m/year. I was responsible for risk assessment and reduction, including pro-active compliance with health and safety regulations, developing a safety conscious working culture for staff and contractors.

KEY SKILL AREAS (COMPETENCIES)

1. **Strategic business planning**
2. **Systems integration, change and project management**
3. **International business co-ordination**
4. **Operational management, planning and control**
5. **Organisation design and change**

EDUCATION AND QUALIFICATIONS

MBA, Open University Business School, 1993–96. Project: *Change management in the Far East.*

ACCA qualified 1984.

BEng (Hons) Manufacturing Engineering with Management. 1976–79, Liverpool University 2:1.

Maths, Physics and Economics GCE 'A' Levels, 11 'O' Levels, St George's School, Newbury.

RECENT TRAINING AND DEVELOPMENT

Globalisation and business ethics (1 day, IOD London, May 2001)

Executive and professional development programme (Eos, March 2000)

International legal compliance for E-Commerce operations (two days, City University, September 2000)

Intranet optimisation (5 days, Oak Tree Systems, June 2000)

Microsoft Office developer's workshop (2 days, February 2000)

ADDITIONAL INFORMATION

Married, 2 children (aged 13 and 16). Good health; non-smoker. Full, clean driving licence.

Willing to relocate within the UK and mobile for short overseas assignments based from UK.

Current interests: sailing; travel; photography. Previous: youth football coach; pilot (PPL).

REFERENCES

Employer references and career development profile available on request.

Appendix 5b Example résumé with experience – competency focused

This résumé uses a competency-based format – sometimes useful for people who want to focus more on their skills, rather than their employment history. It may also be helpful if you are wishing to change career path, or do not want to emphasise your age (see section 7.6).

Douglas Campbell B.Eng. ACCA, MBA.

Business integration and change management

Home phone: 01365-497251
Email: douglh@aaaaaa.com
Mobile: 07684-332779

74 Aylesbury St
WINDSOR
Berkshire SL36 4XX

PROFILE

Production controller, business analyst and change project manager, 8 years' offshore projects engineering in UK plus 12 years' experience with international corporations in IT, telecommunications and distribution, including 6 years in the Middle and Far East.

Specialist skills include project planning and management, financial forecasting and control, business systems integration and corporate restructuring in multicultural management settings. Also harmonising technical and logistic changes with continuity of operations during mergers and project commissioning periods.

Keen team player: innovative, analytical, versatile trouble-shooter. Calm, adaptable, stimulated by periods of crisis or rapid change. Catalyst for change, winning co-operation rather than demanding it. Seeking further strategic change management opportunities at senior management level in high tech business development or corporate restructuring.

KEY SKILL AREAS (COMPETENCIES)

1. Strategic business planning

a) Financial planning for major projects including financing sources during rapid market growth. Projects up to £430 million.

b) Forecasting and co-ordinating contract and investment schedules to ensure self-financing growth through positive cash flows (up to £7.5m).

c) Investment analysis plans, proposals and presentations for major projects eg for a £75m overseas communications centre, office relocation and offshore support contracts.

d) Developing pre- and post-merger financing structures with new parent corporations.

2. Systems integration, change and project management

a) Planning, selection and implementation of new logistics database management systems – from concept to commissioning, eg *Oracle* and *Synthafin v.3*.

b) Planning transitions to fully integrated business systems (purchasing, production and distribution etc) using SAP and transition management methodologies.

c) Upgrading, contingency planning and rehearsal for major risks, eg Y2K compliance project and international Intranet projects.

3. International business co-ordination

a) Experience of running subsidiaries of UK and US companies in UK and the Far East building co-operation between local staff and senior management in regional/global HQs.

b) Induction and strategic guidance for new CEO and Boards of recently acquired subsidiaries. Ongoing liaison, planning and reporting for global HQs.

4. Operational management, planning and control

a) Experience of managing production facilities and operations from middle management to director level setting targets and production schedules. Operating budgets to £15 m/year.

b) Establishing internal financial controls and external compliance including state, European and US regulations and ISO 9000 certification. Compliance with currency regulations.

c) Line management responsibility for staff resources, selection, training and development for up to 250 staff. Direction, co-ordination and motivation of senior supervisors and team leaders. Staff motivation and employee relations, including white- and blue-collar unionised groups. Development, adaptation and implementation of financial policies and procedures associated with corporate changes eg merger and de-merger.

d) Executive responsibility for risk assessment and reduction, including pro-active compliance with health and safety regulations, developing a safety conscious working culture for staff and contractors.

5. Organisation design and change

a) Review of organisation and management structures to identify opportunities for improved efficiency and co-operation plus updating to meet changing markets and business plans.

b) Shared responsibility for all aspects of legal compliance drawing on specialist advice from HQ advisers and external professional advisers.

c) Some experience of directly managing HR and public relations roles in two smaller organisations including government and media contacts.

d) Close involvement as member of senior management teams in strategic plans for internally and externally generated organisation change programmes. Facilitator for change management training and projects with direct input to short term restructuring and longer term company culture change projects.

EMPLOYMENT HISTORY

3/2002–date **Project Planning Director**, *Incubin Telecommunications,* London.

5/98–2/2002 **Corporate Strategy and Contingency Planning Manager**, *Glow-worm Systems,* Slough. Industrial heating control systems.

1/90–3/98 **Project Manager, Business Integration (SAP)**, *Wong Enterprises,* Singapore and Hong Kong, IT component manufacturing.

7/85–11/89 **Business Analyst (Overseas Ventures)**, *NingTel Europe Ltd,* London based + assignments in Egypt, Turkey and Spain.

12/83–6/85 **Offshore Projects Accountant**, *Belltec Engineering,* Aberdeen.

10/79–12/83 **Trainee Project Engineer**, *Belltec Engineering,* Aberdeen. Sub-sea modules

EDUCATION AND QUALIFICATIONS

MBA, Open University Business School, 1993–96. Project: *Change management in the Far East.*

ACCA qualified 1984.

BEng (Hons) Manufacturing Engineering with Management. 1976–79, Liverpool University 2:1.

Maths, Physics and Economics GCE 'A' Levels, 11 'O' Levels, St George's School, Newbury.

RECENT TRAINING AND DEVELOPMENT

Globalisation and business ethics (1 day, IOD London, May 2001)

Executive and professional development programme (Eos, March 2000)

International legal compliance for E-Commerce (2 days, City University, September 2000)

Intranet optimisation (5 days, Oak Tree Systems, June 2000)

Microsoft Office developer's workshop (2 days, February 2000)

ADDITIONAL INFORMATION

Married, 2 children (aged 13 and 16). Good health; non-smoker. Full, clean driving licence. Willing to relocate within the UK and mobile for short overseas assignments based from UK. Current interests: sailing; travel; photography. Previous: youth football coach; pilot (PPL).

REFERENCES

Employer references and career development profile available on request.

Appendix 6
Example of Interview Preparation Table

This Interview Preparation Table (IPT) is based on the résumé in Appendix 4b, and was used for online applications, and for interviews with organisations whose websites identified the main criteria they would use for selection (in the left-hand column). Evidence A was used first, but if already used, it would be referred to, then Evidence B, then C used. The information is recorded in short notes, as a reminder only.

Often one period of employment will provide the strongest evidence. This is fine, but you need to have alternatives in case you are asked to think of a different example. Some pieces of evidence are used for more than one expected question – after all, probably not all expected questions will be asked. You can number each activity in the résumé, and use these numbers in the table if you find this helpful. Refer to Section 10.3 for how to prepare and use this sort of table.

Expected questions	Evidence A	Evidence B	Evidence C
Give me an example of when you had to **set targets**.	**Northern Financial** – I ran the tender process with defined results and time targets.	**Pacific Bank** – I organised test simulations with tight time deadlines.	
Give me an example of when you had to **deliver on targets**.	**Northern Financial** Market Maker incentives – in charge of fee negotiations, I delivered a saving of £500K.	**Army** – I remained effective during extensive sensitive exercises even when v tired, and completed our mission.	**Northern Financial** – produced reports for directors, everyday without fail.

Give me an example of when you had to demonstrate **the self-confidence to tackle unfamiliar problems**.	**Pacific Bank** – I set myself the task of becoming a full member of the team within two months – and succeeded.	**Northern Financial** – I asked to move from IT Purchasing to Product Management, and succeeded despite limited initial knowledge.	
Give an example of when you **'did things your own way'**.	**Northern Financial** – boss was away, I came up with new way of calculating incentives, convinced directors that it was better.	**Running my own company** – no-one else ran a company while still at school. I made it a successful commercial enterprise.	
Give an example of when you **valued everyone regardless of culture or status**.	**Army** – I joined to give me friends outside university, eg electrician, builder. I've always lived in mixed houses. Travelled to gain insight into other cultures.	**Social Services** – representing youth offenders.	
Give an example when you showed your **integrity**.	**Northern Financial** – when all staff were backbiting my boss, I stood up for him.	**Pacific Bank** – I messed up one report, put out correction straight away.	
Give an example of when you demonstrated **clear communication**.	**Northern Financial** – I communicated with the Business Analysts the new product and marketing plans and received vg feedback.	**Univ. Study Group** – I made it clear to everyone that we all had to work together and arranged roles.	

Expected questions	Evidence A	Evidence B	Evidence C
Give an example of when you demonstrated **clarity of argument**.	**Northern Financial** – I persuaded the market makers of the benefits of the new plan.	**Social Services** – representing youth offenders who could not argue for themselves.	**Combined Utilities** – persuading people to switch to CU.
Give an example when you were **decisive**.	**Final Year Project** – I decided on recommendations, and ensured we all committed to them.	**Northern Financial** – decided on the best way to arrange incentives.	
Give an example of when you **dealt with someone different from you**.	**At garden centre**.	**In YHAs while travelling**.	**Pacific Bank** – negotiations with US branch.
Give an example of when you had to **analyse a complex issue**.	**Northern Financial** – I analysed the market and proposed a new way of calculating incentives.	**Pacific Bank** – I analysed the implications for jointly held cards and made recommendations prior to chip and pin launch.	**At Northern Financial and Pacific Bank** I analysed the business until I was accepted as a full member of the team.
Give an example of when you **analysed outside existing boundaries**.	**At university** I worked out a different way to network the PCs in our project so we could communicate directly.	**My own company** – I analysed the market and identified the opportunity before anyone else.	
Give an example when you showed your **imagination**.	**My own company** – I analysed the market and identified the opportunity before anyone else.	**Travel** – I developed my own itinerary and ways to fund my university studies.	

Appendix 7
Interviewer's rating form

Candidate:
Date :

Criteria	Evidence	Rating
Drive (targets,delivery, self-confidence)		
People (difference, honesty, communication decision-making)		
Intellect (analysis, imagination, out-of-the box thinking)		

Remarks:

Recommendation:

Interviewer:

Appendix 8
Example of a 15-document in-tray/e-tray exercise
(See Appendix 9 for a sample response)

FESTIVIA

You have 1.5 hours to consider the following documents. At the end of this time you will see two assessors. They will ask you to present your conclusions in about five to ten minutes, then will ask you questions for about a further 20 minutes.

The country of Festivia has a population of 10 million; it gained independence about 15 years ago, and since then has enjoyed a slowly increasing economic growth which is now about 6% a year. Festivia recently joined the major trading bloc in the region and hopes that will further increase economic growth as trade barriers come down and it has a wider market to sell its goods. Currently average salaries are about $4,000 a year, much less for those still working in the farming sector. About one in three families have a car, most have a motorbike or a cycle, but car ownership is expected to increase significantly over the next ten years. The roads in Festivia have not been well maintained, and a recent World Bank report on Festivia mentioned that poor transport and communication infrastructure is likely to hinder economic growth. Likewise the banking system is not well developed, the Bank of Festivia acts as the central bank issuing bank notes and setting interest rates, currently 5%. The government has a significant influence over the Bank of Festivia, even though it is nominally independent. There are also four commercial banks in Festivia (in one of them, the Fortress Bank of Festivia, the Minister of Finance holds a 30% shareholding), and three international banks including HSBC. The local currency, the Festia, is currently trading at F4=$1US and F7=1UK pound.

Festivia has 100 miles of coastline and has two ports, one of which, Dunich, is the main container and cruise ship port, and the other, Sandatta, is the main bulk, oil and petroleum port. The biggest power station in Festivia is also near Sandatta. Festivia lies in the zone of the world where hurricanes occur, and the mountainous regions of the interior have experienced a few minor earthquakes in recent years. The capital of Festivia is Haimal, named after President Haimal Atoll who has won the last two elections since independence. The name of the capital was changed to Haimal only five years ago.

The military in Festivia is not very well equipped but France, the USA and Britain are all trying to win a large order to re-equip the Festivian army, navy and air force. The Minister of Defence has put a lot of energy into progressing this order, and has been quoted as saying that it is essential for the defence of Festivia against its neighbour Lanstan. There was a military coup about 12 years ago, but after five years there were elections which returned a civilian government headed by Haimal Atoll.

The population of Festivia is comparatively young – earlier wars and poor medical care and water supply meant that many Festivians died before they reached 50, but now children are surviving much longer, and there are increasing numbers of children. This is placing a strain on schools, and there is also a problem of young adult unemployment which currently stands at 25%. There has been some foreign inward investment – in particular Hexagon (the energy and chemical company for which you work) has been considering a new pipeline to carry crude oil over the mountains from Lanstan to the port at Sandatta where it can be transported to refineries in nearby countries and the West. Sungsim, a Korean electronics manufacturer, has set up an assembly plant in Festivia to produce air conditioners and refrigeration units, as well as components for cars. There are some nickel mines in Lanstan, but they are close to being exhausted, and the tribes who owned the land are trying to get compensation for the environmental damage caused to their lands.

Currently all petrol (gasoline), diesel, aviation fuel, power station fuel to generate electricity, and bitumen for roads is brought into Festivia. Hexagon have a distribution terminal at Sandatta from where road tankers deliver fuel to consumers and fuel stations. It is about 40 kilometres from Sandatta to Haimal, and a further 150 kilometres on poor roads, from there to the second largest city in Festivia, Cheong.

There is an American air base near Sandatta, and China has a large embassy in the capital, Haimal. The only newspaper in Festivia, the *Daily Truth* is owned by the Minister of Information; two rival papers have been closed down. The *Daily Truth* reported that this was because of unsafe working conditions in their printing works – the government of Festivia can be particularly vigorous in ensuring safe working conditions in some cases.

The General Manager of Hexagon in Festivia is James Cameron, a 29-year-old business graduate. His job is to ensure that all operations are conducted safely and to a high standard, that good-quality oil and chemicals are provided to the customers in Festivia, to meet annual targets for profitability, to represent the interests of Hexagon in Festivia, and to train Festivian staff to take over the jobs of the two expatriates currently in the positions. One of these positions is his own, that of General Manager. A schematic of some of the main Hexagon staff is shown on the page 202.

You have been assigned to act as the personal assistant to James Cameron for a period of six months as part of a special assignment. You arrived yesterday, and after dinner with two young Festivian graduates, you have reached the office to find a note waiting for you (see page 201).

HEXAGON COMPANY OF FESTIVIA PLC

James Cameron, General Manager

1 January

I am very sorry that I was not there to meet you at the airport, but I hope you enjoyed the dinner with Paul and Chloe last night. I will be out of the country for the next four days at a special meeting of all Hexagon Country Managers, and because we are discussing confidential and sensitive overall company strategy, we are pretty much out of communication for this time. But the next four days are public holidays in Festivia (the President's birthday falls on New Year's Day and this always used to be a public holiday, but this year he announced a second day to celebrate ten years of economic progress). Many of the managers are taking the opportunity to go to their ranches in the interior of Festivia – I am afraid that cell phone coverage is minimal outside the capital area. However, Oscar Reyes, the manager of the Sandatta Terminal, is on duty over the weekend, so if there is anything particularly troubling, you can contact him.

I have also left you on the next page a summary of who is who in the organisation. I had to leave early to get to the conference, so I am afraid there will probably be a pile of mail waiting for you. Penny, my secretary, will have printed it off. Please go through it and use your initiative to take action as necessary. I want you to take whatever action you think is needed before I get back – I do not want to return to find a lot of things just waiting. I would also like to have a general discussion with you about the situation facing Hexagon Festivia, and the business opportunities and threats and any longer term issues you feel are important.

I hope you enjoy your stay in Festivia.

James

General Manager James Cameron (Secretary/PA: Penny Abalfi)				
Terminal Manager	Finance Manager	Health & Safety Manager	Marketing Manager	IT Manager
Oscar Reyes 5 Supervisors 20 terminal staff 50 drivers 1 station renovation	Emily Jones 4 Accountants 5 Finance Assts 12 Billing Assts	Nelson Kadenza 2 H&S Inspectors	Robert Young 2 Advertising Assts 4 order taking	J. Ash

The terminal at Sandatta has 10 tanks and an import/export jetty able to accommodate tankers of up to 40,000 tonnes, as well as a loading gantry able to fill road tankers with products.

Document 1

Hexagon Fuels

Sandatta Fuel Terminal – Daily Report

Tank no.	Product	Maximum capacity (litres)	Capacity (litres) 31 Dec	Capacity (litres) 1 Jan
1	Unleaded petrol	50,000,000	42,123,000	40,861,000
2	Diesel	50,000,000	20,483,000	19,371,000
3	Premium petrol	10,000,000	4,382,000	4,295,000
4	Aviation fuel	50,000,000	22,289,000	21,453,000
5	Heating/power fuel	50,000,000	10,392,000	9,369,000
6	Bitumen	10,000,000	4,024,000	3,972,000
7	Unleaded petrol	50,000,000	0	0
8	Diesel	50,000,000	6,934,000	6,934,000
9	Diesel	50,000,000	27,850,000	27,850,000
10	Aviation fuel	10,000,000	3,456,000	3,456,000

Note: Tank 7 cleaning is proceeding satisfactorily and should be completed by 10th January. The back-up heating on Tank 6 is under repair, but the main heating which uses electricity from the mains is working OK at present. One of the two main pumps which pump fuels from the tanks to the loading gantry is waiting for spare parts (S400D). Tank 6 is a heated tank to prevent the bitumen from hardening in the pipes. Tank 7 is empty and is undergoing its cleaning which is required every two years to avoid an excessive build-up of solids and water in the tank.

Document 2

DAILY TRUTH

1 January

Finance Minister excluded from party to celebrate President's birthday

We hear that David Bestia the Finance Minister was not invited to the President's birthday party yesterday. His staff claimed when we contacted them that the Minister is ill, but he was seen playing tennis earlier in the day – perhaps he sprained his ankle, or his service was letting him down? David Bestia has been travelling outside Festivia a lot recently, meeting other bankers and visiting his villa in Switzerland.

Global warming

From our Environmental Correspondent in Geneva

An international conference held in Geneva recently identified lack of government action in combating global warming – it warned that if action is not taken to reduce the amount of fossil fuels being used, the planet could warm by up to 1.5°C within the next 30 years. This could have a significant effect on populations – for example the polar ice caps could start to melt, increasing sea level by as much as 10 metres and flooding low-lying areas, as well as increasing the sea temperature. This would mean that more areas become prone to cyclones and hurricanes which need a sea temperature in excess of 26°C to have enough energy to start rotating.

Nickel discovery in Lantana

Red River Mining have reported they have found nickel in Lantana – the concession area they have is apparently extensive, and the nickel ore is of good quality. Lantana has no access to the sea, however.

Bright Star Petroleum

Bright Star Petroleum today announced financial results for the last year. Profits increased from F1.2 million last year to F1.4 million this year. The results include the sale of their office in Haimal six months ago. David Bestia owns 50% of the shares in Brave Star.

Document 3

Fortress Bank of Festivia

Current Account

Client: **Hexagon**

Date	Debit (F)	Credit (F)	Balance (F)
20 Dec	700,000		11,500,000
21 Dec		500,000	12,000,000
30 Dec		640,000	12,640,000
30 Dec		200,000	12,840,000
1 Jan			12,840,000
Closing balance			

As requested, we are making arrangements to pay all Hexagon staff salaries into their bank accounts on their normal pay day, ie the first working day of each month.

Document 4

To: All drivers

From: Manager, Health & Safety

Road Safety

I regret to inform you that another delivery to the filling station at Cheong has been hijacked by bandits along the road between Haimal and Cheong. You will be pleased to know that the driver was unhurt, but not before product had been spilled onto the road. We suspect that the bandits are based in Lanstan, and are crossing the border under cover of night.

Nelson Kadenza

Document 5

Weather forecast issued today by the Meterological Office of Festivia, 1 January

---

Strong south-westerly winds are expected to persist over much of the country for the next two days.

Temperatures will remain high, reaching 35°C for much of the time, sea temperature is 26.5°C.

An area of low pressure is forming in the Gulf of Bulalo and is expected to move towards Festivia within the next four days.

Document 6

To: Hexagon Festivia

From: Hexagon Procurement Engineering, London

28 December

Spare Part for Feed Pump S400B
We have finally sourced this spare part, and are arranging for it to be shipped to you. It weighs about 50kg, and in accordance with your standard instructions for heavy items, we are sending it by Value Couriers who have quoted a delivery date of 25 January.

Steve Smith
Procurement Operator

Document 7

Fantastic Festivia Promotions

Robert Young,
Marketing Manager,
Hexagon PLC

Dear Robert,

Special Advertising Campaign

It was good to see you at lunch at the Holly Restaurant last night. I have given the matter some consideration, and would like to propose that we give Hexagon a special series of advertising slots at the forthcoming Cup Final of the Festivian Soccer between Haimal United and Cheong Champions on 1 February. As you know, this event always attracts a huge television audience and we are confident we can negotiate for you a special reduction of 30% on the usual price for such a high-profile event. However, we need to have your response by 3 January at the latest.

With best wishes,

Sammy Justian
General Manager

Document 8

Lantana Liberty

We give you warning that if you do not pay the sum of F20,000 we will attack one of your road tankers in the next 2 days, and set it on fire.
You have been warned!!!

If you agree to our terms, place an advertisement in the next edition of the Daily Truth, saying:
'For Sale – Surplus office equipment F1000', and give an email address. We will contact you.

Victory to the Liberators of Lantana!

Document 9

Transport Union of Festivia

30 December

Brothers: We have again submitted our just pay claim to the Management of Brave Star Petroleum and they have again rejected it. As you see from our calculations the current pay rates are only 90% of what they were 5 years ago once we take into account the increases in cost of living which is currently running at 5%. The rates of pay are already 5% below that paid by Hexagon. If there is no positive response from management by 2 January, we will have no alternative but to recommend an all out strike of all workers employed by Brave Star, and to prevent all deliveries from the terminal at Sandatta.

Document 10

Delivery Notice

US Air Force Base, Sandatta

30 December

We confirm receiving your order for 1,000,000 litres of aviation fuel on an urgent basis as Bright Star are unable to deliver. We confirm that our standard specification for aviation fuel is for a maximum of 0.00001% water. The delivery will be made on 2 January by road tanker.

Hexagon Orders Supervisor,
Sandatta Terminal

Document 11

Festivia Building Corporation

Marketing Manager,
Hexagon Festivia

Dear Robert,

Upgrades and Renovation of Fuel Stations in Festivia

We are pleased to enclose our quote for a complete renovation of a further four fuel stations in Festivia, located as shown on the plan, and to the specifications you indicated. Our total price would be F2,000,000/station, payable 50% on start of work, a further 30% on completion of the civil engineering work, and the remaining 20% on final completion as determined by our engineers.

We would need your agreement to this price by 5 January, otherwise the price would increase by 2%.

We look forward to doing business with you.

Pedro Palanga
Construction and Contracts Manager
Cc James Cameron

Document 12

Telephone Message left on the voicemail of James Cameron

Date: 30 December, 10.45 pm

Mr Cameron, this is Manuel Osaga, duty Supervisor at the Terminal, you should be aware that Pump S400A is vibrating a lot. I have asked our maintenance crew to look at it tomorrow, and I will keep you informed. I have also left a message with Mr Reyes.

Document 13

Shipping Movements

Hexagon Supply and Trading, Houston

Hexagon Glory, carrying 20,000 tonnes fuel products, was scheduled to arrive Sandatta Terminal, eta 4 January, now diverted to Tradoria.

Document 14

Sandatta Laboratory

Tests carried out on fuels as part of your normal quality assurance programme.

Tank	% water	% solids
1	0.00000	0.0001
2	0.00001	0.0003
3	0.00002	0.0002
4	0.00006	0.00011
5	0.00000	0.0001
6	0.00001	0.00003
7	0.00001	0.000045
8	0.00002	0.00002
9	0.00001	0.00001
10	0.00001	0.00002

Document 15

Voicemail for James Cameron

Hello, this is the hospital at Haimal. I have to inform you that Oscar Reyes has just been admitted to hospital with chest pains. He is currently under sedation in our private ward.

Message left at 31 December.

Appendix 9
Example response to the in-tray exercise

There are a number of urgent matters that require immediate action, and sometimes careful longer term consideration to prevent future problems recurring, and to ensure that strategic opportunities are seized.

Urgent issues

I would see if there is a secretary or administrator (probably Penny if she is available) who can help me action the following:

* Aviation fuel for the US Air Force: the water content of Tank 4 which we have been using yesterday and would presumably use today unless action is taken is 6x over specification, and could cause a major disaster if the water freezes at high altitude. I would call the duty supervisor, explain my position, and ensure that they are aware of the lab results and to only use Tank 10 for aviation fuel.

* Oscar Reyes is in hospital but there is no word as to whether anyone has notified his wife. I would phone the hospital to find out if they have notified her. If not, I would phone her myself, explain my position, and ask the terminal to arrange for a driver to take her to the hospital.

* With Oscar Reyes hospitalised, I would ask who is the senior supervisor who can deputise for him. I would also ask who is the alternate duty manager, and notify them accordingly.

* I would ask the duty supervisor to liaise with the Health and Safety Manager and then brief all drivers on the threats we have received, and ask them to take appropriate action. I would ask them to contact the police and the US base to see if they can provide an escort for the fuel.

* There are only two feed pumps to the terminal. S400B is waiting for spare parts and S400A has just started to vibrate badly. If S400A fails then the terminal cannot operate – we can supply no products to our customers, which would be very serious. I would phone or email Hexagon Procurement and ask them to send the spare part for S400B as soon as possible, not by Value Couriers.

* The advertising campaign – I would ask Robert Young to ensure that he responds in time, but not to be overly pressured by what seems to be an artificial deadline. Similarly I would ask him to contact Festivia Building to insist that the artificial deadline they impose be suspended at least until James Cameron is back.

* I would advise the duty supervisor that Brave Star workers are likely to try to prevent deliveries from our terminal. They should brief drivers not to be diverted, and the Health and Safety Manager to request the local police to be on hand to ensure safe passage.

Less urgent but important issues

* The sea temperature is above that required for a cyclone (26°C), and the Hexagon tanker has been diverted – possibly for this reason. I would ask for a meeting of the most senior representative of each division to review what action we should take if a cyclone appears likely to hit Festivia. For example, how high is the terminal above sea level, have cyclones hit before, can we move the road tankers to a safe (higher) location? Can we shut down the terminal and are any staff required to stay there, and if so, how is their safety to be ensured? Where is our IT data stored, how can its integrity be ensured? J. Ash should be looking into this if not already. I would ask the duty supervisor to consider the impact of the diversion of the tanker – how many days can we continue to supply product?

* I would ask Hexagon why they diverted the tanker, and when the next delivery is expected.

* The terrorist threat – I would ask the Health and Safety Manager to inform the local police and request heightened security, but otherwise no action. We would certainly not take the action they request.

* I would ask the Marketing Manager to consider the possibilities of supplying fuels and lubricants to the nickel operation in Lantana.

* The Fortress Bank where we seem to have a large part of our funds may be at risk – the Finance Minister seems to be falling out of favour, and his Brave Star brand seems to be failing (the only profit increase came from selling their office). I would ask the Finance Manager to take steps to minimise our exposure in a discreet way. I would also ask the Marketing Manager to consider the opportunities raised by a possible collapse of Brave Star, and whether there is any merit in bidding for Brave Star ourselves. We also need to prioritise this against the renovation of our stations.

* The oil find in Lantana – a pipeline across Festivia gives us lots of strategic opportunities including building a refinery in Festivia to add value to the oil, and supply other countries in the trading zone.

Appendix 10
Example of a Presentation Exercise

You are asked to consider the effect of a trebling (3x) in the price of crude oil from its present level. What impact would this have on this organisation, what changes if any should at least be considered, and what are the priorities? Are there any opportunities that should be seized? What are the wider strategic implications of this trebling in the cost of crude oil? You are not expected to know detailed technical considerations, but you are expected to indicate the areas that need to be considered in as much detail as you can.

Please take 30 minutes to consider this, then make a presentation to two assessors for about five to ten minutes, after which they will ask you questions about your presentation. You may use PowerPoint on the PC provided, or the flip chart in the room if you wish.

Appendix 11
Example of a group task

You are all part of a special project group brought together to propose the best way to strengthen this organisation's brand amongst people aged 20 to 30. The Marketing Director has asked for this since you are likely to have first-hand knowledge of what needs to be done. She is prepared to consider all ideas you put forward, but obviously the more there are the less impact each will have. She is also prepared to make available funding, but would want to have at least some indications of what you see as the benefits that will be gained, and the actions that would be involved. You are not expected to have detailed financial or technical knowledge of these costs. However, you should be able to indicate the areas in which work will be required, and the likely scope.

You are each asked to spend five minutes considering your own ideas, then have a general discussion for 40 minutes. At the end of this time your group will be asked to make a short (five minute) presentation on your proposals. You can organise yourselves as you wish.

The general discussion will be observed by two managers, who will make notes but will probably not take part in the discussion. After the presentation they may well ask you questions for a further 25 minutes.

Appendix 12
Useful sources

In most cases I have shown the websites, as it is usually quicker and cheaper to check these out to decide which is useful for you. Most sites have book(s) or other documents identified in the site.

Competency-based résumés, Robin Kessler and Linda Strasburg. Career Press, 2005. *www.careerpress.com* A clear source if you specifically want to write a competency-based résumé.

Résumés for First Time Job Hunters, the editors of McGraw-Hill. McGraw-Hill, 2005. About 100 example résumés from early job hunters. Very US oriented.

What color is your parachute? Richard Boles. California: Ten Speed Press 2006. Its associated website is *www.jobhuntersbible.com*. A comprehensive book and website.

www.goldjobs.com and *www.silverjobs.com* Sites for high-paying high-impact jobs and job seekers.

www.monster.com and *www.monster.co.uk* Big job posting sites for USA and UK.

www.yahoo.com or *www.uk.careers.yahoo.co.uk* Another job site for USA and UK.

www.hays.com Large recruitment agency site covering UK, European and US jobs.

www.reed.co.uk Largest UK job site, full of useful information.

www.businessculture.com Good advice on business culture and etiquette in most countries. Requires payment (about $24).

www.eurograduate.com/marketreports/culture-matters Neat, short summaries of what to expect in the different European countries.

www.geert-hofstede.com Professor Hofstede could be called the 'grandfather' of business cross-cultural studies, and conducted one of the earlier surveys which identified five dimensions which vary between cultures: Power-Distance; Individualism; Masculinity; Uncertainty Avoidance; Long-term Orientation.

www.eoslifework.co.uk Useful site by professional career counsellor Dai Williams.

www.shldirect.com provides example psychometric tests (ability and personality) and gives some feedback. They also provide some career advice from a link at *www.shl.com*

www.acpeople.com.au AC People, an Australian search and selection agency offering free online advice.

www.careersonline.com.au Careers on Line, an Australian agency with professional careers advice.

www.jobstar.org A USA site that contains 200+ profession-specific salary surveys and links to 300 more.

www.vault.com A predominantly USA site that aims to provide 'insider' advice on work in mainly financial organisations, and hints on how to apply.

www.k-state.edu/acic/career/options A USA site from the University of Kansas, useful for showing the type of work that graduates with various degrees tend towards.

www.belbin.com The main website for Dr Belbin's work on team roles.

www.ppc.sas.upenn.edu Professor Martin Seligman was already a well-established psychology professor in Pennsylvania studying learned helplessness when I was researching evolutionary psychology at Bryn Mawr College nearby. Professor Seligman is now a leading expert in positive psychology or happiness. This and related websites will give a good insight into the field.

If you have any comments or questions about this book or your own experience, email me at *andymgibb.yahoo.co.uk*

Acknowledgements

Many people contributed to this book, and I owe thanks to all of them. It is impossible to name everyone, so this is a small representative selection only, and my apologies to those not included here. My thanks go to you nonetheless. This book is based on years of developing and running training courses, especially in the Shell Global Recruitment Team. My thanks are especially due to Tony Shaw and the Shell recruiters, who although not psychologists provided significant creativity and feedback during the recruitment and selection process. Mark Wade, Tim Luker, Sven Gudde, Peter Ashford, Tom Pere, Hans Wierde, Geoff Brown and Helen Woolsey especially spring to mind but the whole team in London, the Hague, Houston and Melbourne deserve credit. Nicole Cunningham-Snell in particular continued much of the research in this field, and is now developing it further in leadership development as a manager and psychologist.

Richard Scriven introduced many of the early assessment exercises, and Jelle Kiesling wholeheartedly welcomed the early introduction of assessment centre techniques to recruitment for the SMDS plant in Bintulu, Malaysia. Dai Williams read the career choice chapters and gave helpful input, and several friends contributed résumés for use as examples. My thanks to them, although I have promised they will remain anonymous.

The team at Ernst and Young International based in New York and London were instrumental in enabling the final chapters; my thanks especially to John Cornish, Jill Lounsbury and Andrew Jones. James my son made several excellent contributions from his own experience, and read the draft, and my wife Nicky also read the draft and helped with improvements. Nikki Read has been a gracious and efficient publisher and a great help even when communicating over half a world and myriad time zones away. However, the final version and any omissions or inaccuracies are my responsibility. Please email me at *andymgibb@yahoo.co.uk* if you wish to comment on any part.

Andy Gibb

Kent, UK and 'Intrepid of Dover', Australia

Index